DISCLAIMER

"How to Make More Money – Strategies for Financial Freedom" is intended for general information and entertainment purposes only. It is <u>NOT</u> intended to give accounting, banking or legal advice. It is understood that that there are no guarantee implied or otherwise.

Each person financial circumstance and situation is different and individualized. Before implementation of any financial, banking or legal changes, reference must be made to your personal certified accountant, banking profession, attorney or any relevant professional or advisor.

The Author, publisher, family and associates of "How to Make More Money – Strategies for Financial Freedom" formally advise that they are <u>not</u> – in any form or fashion – acting as an agent or have accepted the position of your personal accountant, banking profession , attorney, consultant or advisor.

Each person reading, listening or using "How to Make More Money – Strategies for Financial Freedom" accepts full responsibility and risk for changes in their personal or business financial, banking or legal circumstances and for any losses or gains incurred.

The author, publisher , family and associates of "How to Make More Money – Strategies for Financial Freedom" specifically denies and disclaim any and all liability caused by reading, hearing or the use of the information contain therein or any related seminars conducted by the author or any representative

The reader, user and listener of this book "How to Make More Money – Strategies for Financial Freedom" , agree to completely indemnify the author, publisher, family and associates against any and all claims, any litigation, any monetary claims due to losses or gains in their personal finances.

The author , publisher , family and associates specifically disclaims any and all liability that results from the use , application of any and all principles, methodologies , models or any/all information contained in this book.

This book is NOT intended to give legal, accounting, banking, investment, consulting or any basic or professional advice.

All names and business references are meant only to promote clarity; however are all **fictional descriptions** and not actual individuals or businesses (names).

HOW TO MAKE MORE MONEY

Strategies for Financial Freedom

In appreciation of my Beautiful, Amazing, Wonderful & intelligent wife for her love and support during past eleven years. She is a true gift and blessing from God, without her vision, patience and confidence in me this book would not have been possible.

God grants us blessings seen and unseen - Our two daughters are our joy and true centre of happiness.

A special note of thanks to my mother, friend, beacon and strength – thanks for not giving up on me. To my brothers and sister – you uniqueness contributes so much to my life.

There have never been such a great and loving family who accepted me without boundaries – thanks to Pastor Goundan & family.

Written in memory of my father and mentor Ganesh Siewdass (dec'd)

Want to listen to Live Seminars online?

Visit our Website

www.topmoneyplan.com

Preface

Welcome to How To More Money, Strategies for Financial Freedom.

The purpose of this book is to point you in the right direction, provide sound education and affirmatively place you on the cutting edge of financial mastery. In an effort to make you financially successful, a concerted effort has also been made to germinate ethical and moral values to support the human spirit. It is envisioned that simplistic ideas can be the catalyst for a change in thinking, direction and ultimately success.

We live in uncertain times and knowledge becomes power, this book has been designed to open your eyes to the immense world of business, finance and money. Both novice and professionals can benefit as we seek to bridge the gap and reveal well kept secrets of the financially elite.

This book attempts to feed the minds of people who wish to break free of their financial valleys and help to carves new directions in the soul and heart. It is envision that with a contented heart your first million will be a walk in the park.

Praise to my Lord and Savior Jesus Christ for planting in me the vision and knowledge to write this book.

In loving appreciation of my beautiful wife and daughters for their love and support during the past 11 years.

Curtis Siewdass

Table of Content

The Foundation

		Page
Chapter 1	Dodging the bullet	9
Chapter 2	The Missing Link	11
Chapter 3	Putting Family First	13
Chapter 4	How to see Money?	15
Chapter 5	What do you Know?	17

Starting your business

Chapter 6	Business Entities	20

The Tools

Chapter 7	Focus (CS Model)	23
Chapter 8	Technology	27
Chapter 9	Staffing & Training (CGS Method)	30

Financials

Chapter 10	Setting up your Accounts (Cash Model)	34
Chapter 11	The two businesses	38
Chapter 12	Understanding of Business Models	43
Chapter 13	Financial Software	49
Chapter 14	Power of Compounding	51
Chapter 15	Understanding Interest Flow Cycle & Investments	53
Chapter 16	Interest Flow Cycle & Investments – Practical application	57
Chapter 17	Offshore Business & Conversion Advantages	62

Marketing

Chapter 18	Differences between Wants & Needs	68
Chapter 19	How people think & behave?	72
Chapter 20	Branding	76
Chapter 21	Statistic vs. Results	79

Chapter 22   Phased Marketing   83

Plan to fail

Chapter 23   P2F   91

Strategies

Chapter 24   Strategies   100

Chapter 25   How to see your Global Business?   113
Chapter 26   Bonus Chapter –
              The Power of Processes   116
Chapter 27   Conclusion   122
Chapter 28   Epilogue   125

~ The Foundation ~

Chapter 1
Dodging the bullet

The bullet whizzed past narrowly missing his forehead – he threw his body onto the pavement hoping the rounds had stopped. Several days later the trauma still had not subsided.

In many situations, our life seems to dictate the above example - narrow misses that predominantly govern our financial stature. Many people suffer due to the lack of financial literacy and understanding. A great proportion of failures stems from the inability to find monetary solutions for daily challenges. Resources are used up leaving financial derelicts across every spectrum of life.

This chapter will identify basic flaws common to most individuals and highlight those things which keep them from attaining real and sustained financial success. To the untrained mind, these principles may appear insignificant however they guide the quality of your life towards fruitfulness and joy. If money is attained without these vital changes, it leads to the daily degeneration of life. The importance of this chapter is paramount to all subsequent principles taught and should peak the urgency for change.

Most lottery winners become poor in a very short time due to an inability to become students of their own behavior or learn who they really are inside. The addition of money only elevates the innate desire to gain recognition and authority brought about by the mighty dollar.

The basic rule
Habits + Money => Success or Failure

Habits developed in life will follow when you attain the first million. A person whose behavior is erratic will be an erratic millionaire and lose their money extremely quickly.

This recurring mistake is made by most individuals; they willingly or unknowingly ignore alarm bells and enter into a callous state of operation. At this stage very little positive things affect values or habitual routines.

In an effort to further clarify our formula, the following are just a few examples that will expand your view. It is hoped the awareness of these will synergize momentous behavioral changes to sustain financial freedom.

Alcohol

It is a known fact adults engage in casual drinking to ease the stress, bond with colleagues and politically cling glasses at dignified events. While moderation may not be harmful- individuals who engage in excess alcoholic consumption develop a habitual appetite for the intoxicating feeling.

Alcohol mingled with available money and the craving for booze will transform into a full blown addiction. If you are thinking this may not be you – how often do you visit pubs to relax? This will give an indication of the progression of your free time, money and life expectancy.

What effect will this have on the accumulation of money? The only way to get the booze is to spend money. Subsequently the mental and physical discipline required to make money will be non-existent.

Bad Temper & Impatience

The most detrimental thing in acquiring wealth is an inability to control one's emotional state of mind. This causes compounded problem at home, work and with network of friends.

It is so infectious; the habitual tantrum turns into a ravenous appetite for control. While wealth may stay in tact, you will be a very lonely corpse – six feet under. The purpose of wealth is to improve the quality of life, not sprout people with lesser moralistic behaviors.

Sex and Infidelity

In the right marital setting sex is a wonderful thing. A rich person who engages in infidelity gets addicted and loose not only money but morality. A human void of morality is a time bomb of degradation, with no respect for themselves or humanity.

Infidelity absorbs money like a sponge and results in a dishonest existence. These behaviors will not support increased cash flow or wealth.

This list is by no means conclusive and varies according to the individual. The lesson to be learnt is to live life with a Godly "clear conscience". Always aim for self progression that leads to a better quality of life for all.

The best rule
Good Habits + Money = Success

Chapter 2
The Missing Link
(Big mistake of success)

The funeral took place on Thursday afternoon at 2 pm, everyone and anyone attended this event. The car park was screaming for the service to be over. Those who could not fit in the church searched tirelessly for every crevice that captured a glimpse of his face.

He was adored by politicians, business men, families and vagrants. He represented a complete example of a beautiful soul. His careful gentleness was only exceeded by the size of his heart. Every day of his life was a joyful experience, as he pursued happiness in everyone he touched. As you entered his plush office inlaid with chrome trimming. A simple picture on the wall read - *"A life of service"*. Every visitor or employee was treated with respect and hospitality, every critic was converted with a smile.

The event concluded on time, family and close friend proceeded to his home to pay homage. At the house they all speculated the cause of his death, heart attack, diabetes, brain tumor. The questions continued like an addictive wave flooding the entire the room.

A five year old child had been listening to the adult dilemma grew tired of all the clamoring. With his innocent intelligence shouted, maybe he was too fat! No one paid attention. A more aggressive impatience he shouted again, he was too fat!

As the sound of his voice resounded, the room grew silent. His mother realizing his disrespect and blasphemy promptly scolded him into silence. After the sobering discipline, the room continued to converse ignoring the blatant truth that was revealed.

Missing Link

There are thousands of business people who make money daily and deliberately ignore the foundation stone supporting their wealth. This foundation forms the basic building blocks for life. Despite the importance, it is the most ignored aspect of our daily schedule.

The missing link I am referring to is your *Health*. The accumulation of wealth or financial freedom would not be possible without health. The trend is to focus on making money and not health. The doctorial culprits are the business community who use intelligence to make money. They seldom use the same skill to enhance their health or daily lives. The story highlights the greatness we can achieve and the suffering faced due to ill health.

Money cannot replace your life; –Most wealthy individual have the misconception money makes you live longer. This error is made due to a dependence on money for their daily comfort and need. A link is made in the brain and heart that money can solve any problem. It does not matter the size of your wallet, it will never replace your life. The purpose of wealth is to increase the standard of living for ourselves, family, friend and associates. Never make money your God.

Money will never replace the proper use of your organs; - Wealth brings enjoyment and fulfillment however can furnish life with wanton excess. This goes unnoticed until our health begins to visible deteriorate or our doctor informs us that we have developed a severe medical condition. Sometimes it is too late to reverse the condition. Life is forced to change in ways that are beneath your expected standard of living. Don't let gluttony be a guide to enjoyment, it will only lead to your voluntary demise.

Money does not prevent fat deposits in the arteries; - It does not matter how wealthy you are, fat or cholesterol WILL NEVER respect a bank account. The more you eat the quicker you will die. Excessive eating leads to overweight. This poses an increasing risk for dangerous and

15

degenerative conditions. We need to make a conscious effort to develop better eating habits.

Money is useless when you are have a heart attack or stroke; - Money cannot help you during a heart attack or stroke. What good is money if you cannot enjoy life or are paralyzed? Would you prefer a life of health or Long term illness?

Money will not ease your families' pain when you are bed ridden; - Money may pay for excellent medical care. It will not comfort your family while you are on a hospital bed. It will not prevent them from being worried and saddened by your health.

Money will not comfort your family when you are gone; - How much money will ease a family's grief if you die? Will the dollar bill be able to speak to your spouse? Will the bank account be able to hug your children when they are crying? Put life and money in the right perspective.

The basic lesson to be learnt is to develop the right perspectives and priorities. This will ensure consistent and everlasting wealth. Life is a gift to be enjoyed, make the right steps today so you can enjoy future rewards.

Chapter 3
Putting your family first

The most gut wrenching thing to do is to start a business. The process will test every fiber of your being. It can demolish the weak hearted soul who is unprepared to acquire knowledge. The negatives are often scary and intimidating however the benefits outweigh the financial oasis that lay beyond minor challenges. A business is a great achievement for anyone, it sprout emotional muscles thought to be unattainable. Businesses sprout enthusiasm, customer service and professionalism in the brains of successful entrepreneurs.

The untrained or uninformed spend an immense amount of time trying to develop a model that is profitable and globally expansive. The illusion of "not enough time" develops in those people who build with no focus on business systems. Their modes operandi is a never-ending race leading to stress and medical deterioration. As time progresses, to *'them'* the day becomes shorter and the minutes mover faster.

Building a business creates an imaginary urgency to spend time away from home and personal lives. It forces the investment of time to make more profits. The initial phase of a new business requires time. It it is not a predominant rule and not the goal of millionaires. They tirelessly search for methods and systems that reduce their workload and works in their absence.

Priorities
A new genre of profit minded intellect has been schooled in the fine art of profit margin, variances and return on investments. While this forms the basis for cash flow and equity acquisitions, it does not gear towards life

improvements. If this drive goes unchecked individuals are led by money and not towards a better quality of life.

It does not matter the complexities of our present nuclear family. Its purpose is the same all over the world. It does not matter if blood relatives or foster units. They contribute to an emotional impression on the heart, values and efficiency of the brain. This consciousness is divinely inspired and imprinted from birth. It forms a foundation stone, a pedestal and a center from which greatness springs.

A blind focus on monetary things breaches our foundational truths. We find more reasons to be away from our families than focus on improving their lives and ours.

We must never forget that we are human beings. We need human tenderness and touch to pump our glory and elevate our wings. They may expose your weaknesses with a full helping of candor and you may question their sanity. In most cases they are led by love and an honest need to see you prosper.

When reference is made to family, it lies in the context of the immediate family. The individuals seen when one arrives to their palace or humbly abode. It does not mean to lavish spending on all extended family. You will soon marry an empty bank account with no hope for divorce. When assisting extended family member ensure the monetary help fits the loving need. Do not become someone's money tree. Let your conscience be a guide and ensure decisions are aligned with continuity of money and not prophesied bankruptcy.

We must put family first and spend time enjoying their laughter, pain or moodiness. It builds relationships and cannot be quantified by profit charts. It is the simple art of coexist and flourishing with others. When priority is placed on family first, the effort of making money becomes more rewarding. A happy family contributes to a joyful person. This joy can almost guarantee a life of wealth and business.

A person can be very successful without much interference from the immediate family. The downstream effect of this deliberate isolation is apparent and tangible. What is the use of earning all that money and no loved ones to share it with? We earn money to gain a better quality of life and enhance the lives of those we love. To do otherwise defeat the essence of life it self: - *"to love and to be loved"*.

A business owner must maximize time spent with their families by developing adequate systems that can work independently. A simple example is to set appointments that do not conflict with family time. This example is very simplistic and might seem insignificant. It will generate momentum giving your effort stability.

The real goal it asking this pertinent question, ***"How can I make more money while improving my family life"***. I recommend you write down a minimum of 25 -50 practical things that specifically addresses the question. The reason is to create a solutions bank which can be referenced at any time.

The result is that your intellect will change from being money oriented to family centered. This is a very good thing and is the first step to move your business from being a small dot on the map to a multi –million dollar industry.

Do not read any further until you have honestly assessed and are aware of who represents family. Is your affection or lack thereof impacting on the greatness that family?

Chapter 4
How to see Money?

The average person lives from paycheck to paycheck and often dream of a bonus or raise in salary. The idea of wealth boils down to winning the lottery or acquiring a loan. The dollars are meticulously counted to ensure food is on the table, utilities are paid and basic needs are met. There is little left over for entertainment, saving, car repairs or God forbid – medical bills.

An illusion exists that excess money, being financially free and wealthy is only for the rich and famous. The average Joe learns the necessity of money but seldom think they are capable of moving beyond that comfort zone.

In reality many families are living below the poverty line and struggling to make ends meat. The resulting heartache and depression heavily impacts upon the daily joys. It often leads to alcoholism and drug abuse to deal with the pressures.

The dismal story is more common than you think. People are proud and often ashamed of their financial situation, the reality is rarely revealed. The general population is either oblivious to the hardships or deliberately become callous to the cause.

I am not referring only to the poor but the middle class, the 9-5 working class. Money is a constant juggling event, the larger the family the more difficult it becomes. The working class often scrapes the bottom of the financial barrel to meet needs. The influx of salary is short lived and resources dry quickly. The eager wait for the next salary begins, *tic toc, tic toc.*

The change begins when you see money in a completely different way. It is **not** only for the rich but can be attained by anyone. The difference between a multi-millionaire and the average person on the street is how they see money. The multi-millionaire is very confident they can make money. The average person is afraid to change historical beliefs.

The purpose of this chapter to create a vision that anyone can be a millionaire. This vision is imperative to your journey and unless it is believed money is attainable this book will be useless. The right mindset starts with seeing the future in a completely different way and committing the intellect to believe in the multi-millionaire status.

It is not some complex procedure or one hundred page manual. It is simple seeing yourself with one, two or ten million dollars. The hardest thing faced is the idea of attaining larger sums of money. Every fiber of their being fights the thought and defends the lack of money as destiny. The proposal spontaneously cause profuse comments; - are you mad?", "are you crazy?" or my favorite "what are you smoking?".

It is very simple to change how you see money. Think about it daily; the quality of life, amount of money and vacations etc. Money must be seen long before it becomes reality. It is a general rule, *"what the mind can envision often becomes reality"*. There are so many successful people who had a dream, followed simplistic ideas and earns millions every month. It does not matter if you are a janitor or a CEO of a mega industry, being a millionaire start with a picture envisioned in your heart and mind.

We must give ourselves the permission to have daily dreams and each day make the picture clearer and clearer. Endeavor to back up dreams with factual research and the acquisition of extensive information in the chosen business field. The more exposure to the vision the more our heart, mind and body becomes congruent to the goal. New directions will form pathways in the brain and produce a drive towards achieving the desired goal.

I am not trying to confuse you with semantics or give the false impression that one can achieve anything with a thought. I may want to lift a plane over my head but reality

21

forces me to accept that I will be crushed in seconds. The basic idea is to form a mental foundation via dreams, visions and thoughts. This process produces a base that springs ideas, procedures and systems. These are combined with qualified research and factual information. It will form the start of your millionaire business. Let's get down to business- how is this done?

- Create a list of 25 business ideas.
- Choose the top 5 ideas.
- Rate each of the 5 ideas – give them a value (1-10) (ex. Idea 5 = 9)
- Choose the top rated idea
- Picture our self 5 years in the future – would you want to be doing this 5 years from now.
- Think about the business daily
- Do research.
- Collect information.

This simple procedure will start the mental wheels of your business and give the fire to start. If you are prepared to convert those dreams into reality continue reading. If you are having difficulty seeing a clear picture, reread this chapter a couple of times until your brain sees with clarity.

Chapter 5
What do you know?

As we continue to form foundation stones for the business owner, it imperative not only envision the finale, but be equipped to handle the journey. Entrepreneurs mistake ambition for skill; while gusto may drive a temporary influx of cash it does not sustain longevity or business growth. The resulting businesses implode onto it self and the fallout can be very expensive.

It is sometimes very difficult to convince a person they lack skill to operate a business. The person being coached erroneously takes new suggestion as an attack to their personality and an assault on their capability. When this mental wall goes up, it is almost impossible to impart new ideas or systems.

Historical beliefs, values and cultural exposure are some of the culprits. People gravitate and weld themselves onto archaic ideas which produce little cash flow. Beliefs are held so tightly very few people change. This is one of the major reasons new businesses open and quickly close.

Individuals do not willingly sabotage themselves however *"work very hard"* instead of *"working very smart"*. They believe nothing compares to *"good old sweat and elbow grease"*. Do not misunderstand the statement, it simple means the daily operation of a business becomes priority rather than the acquisition of new skills. The owner's skill will ultimately dictate profit and growth of any enterprise.

There are so many street vendors who can become CEO's of mega industries, however limit the intake of new ideas, methods and systems. This heavily impacts on one's intellect and money making abilities. It causes concentration on *"quick street cash mentality"* instead of cash flow. A person is destined to remain a street vendor unless significant change takes place in the brain to

23

jumpstart new directions. This thought process exists in all strata's and crosses industry borders. It limits the growth of very skilled persons who would otherwise be financially free and wealthy.

People become wealthy as a result of knowledge, experience and common sense; not only academics. A person may have done very poorly in school, however is very wealthy because of an open mind and a veracious appetite for knowledge. It can be said *"knowledge is power"*. I have restated this into a more practical application - *"Structured knowledge opens the mind to produce great power"*. Knowledge by itself is worthless unless placed against facts and quality research. These form unbreakable bonds sprouting professionalism and money.

The purpose of this chapter is to provide basic awareness of business knowledge and the necessity for competence. Prior to opening your business, it is recommended spending 6 months to 1 year acquiring knowledge in the chosen field. Acquiring pertinent information will be pivotal to your profit and sustainability. In order for a person to speak the language of business, they must have an understanding of marketing, finance and technology.

- Marketing – The ability to convince the wider population to desire the benefits of your product or service and make a decision to purchase.

- Finance – The complete tracking and measurement of budget, cash flow and profits.

- Technology – A software program, methods or ideas which enables increased efficiency and results in more profits.

To acquire knowledge one can read books, great author have researched thousands of topics and presented into easy to understand formats. Good authors provide unique

24

interpretations on existing facts and a step by step guide to increase the knowledge bank.

While nothing compares to reading a good business book, audio tapes on related topics can speed up the acquisition of knowledge. It enables repetition and provides an interactive experience. It does not matter the method chosen, make a decision now. Go on a daily journey to acquire knowledge and see your profit break through the roof.

Remember the quote *"Structured knowledge opens the mind to produce great power"*. This power, confidence and motivation are integral tools for life and making money.

Starting
~ Your business ~

Chapter 6
Business Entities

Mary and Joe are vegetarians and delighted in coming up with great recipes to excite their palates. There were meal plans for each day of the week which included scrumptious deserts and an everlasting flow of fruit smoothies. They enjoyed entertaining and regularly invited close likeminded friends to enjoy their passion. The word quickly spread and the once small get-together turned into a bi-weekly vegetarian extravaganza. These events become so popular non-vegetarians soon attended the feast.

Frank, a regular attendee and a very close friend to Mary and Joe sat poolside. He surveyed the two hundred plus guest who were lining up to fill their plate with vegetarian food. Being a very astute person he quickly recognized an income opportunity for himself, Mary and Joe. Arriving home approximately 8pm, he gave the couple a phone call. On speaker phone the three reminisce the evening and were contented to have maintained friendship over fifteen years.

Mary noticed the excitement in Frank's voice and enquired – what is on your mind Frank? Hesitating at first, he recounted his observation; why don't we open a vegetarian restaurant? There was a short silence as the thought sunk into the friends' minds. That is a great idea replied Joe; I will be the accountant, Frank you will be the CEO and Mary will be the temp. Mary, realizing she was the center of the joke quickly gave Joe a tap upside his head. The three friends met on a Thursday afternoon at Frank's home to discuss the details.

The three visit their local government department and opened "Exotic Vegetarian Delights". The relevant forms were completed and the minimal fee was paid. A visit was made to the bank and a company's account was opened – Mary, Joe and Frank *Trading as "Exotic Vegetarian*

Delights". No one realized the restaurant was opened as "sole traders" and not a limited liability company.

Things were going well for approximately six months and the bank deposits were racking up. Customers were fighting for reservation at this exclusive palace. The cook had to go on some emergency leave and a temporary replacement was hired. He came well recommended (so they thought); this was his fifth job in two years. He was good at hiding flaws and quickly left the prior companies before trouble started. Needless to say, a few customers at Exotic Vegetarian Delights fell severely ill from food poisoning.

The three friends were contacted by a law firm advising that the restaurant was being sued for the incident. The damages requested were five hundred thousand dollars. In a strange twist of events, the judge awarded a total of fifty thousand dollars to the victims, the money was quickly paid.

The litigation taught a valuable lesson. The friends contacted their attorney and accountant. A new company _"Exotic Vegetarian Delights limited"_ was opened. Acting on the advice of the professionals they also opened separate companies for future restaurants thus limiting their liability and protecting their bank account from legal claims.

In the business world one of the most important legal structures is the choice of entities. This dictates the level of risk and how well protected the assets of the company are from those seeking to make an easy buck. Newbie's tend to conduct business as a sole trader or partnership and seldom consider the legal responsibility or ramifications of doing business. Legal consequences can and will expose you to unlimited liability and completely demolish money making efforts.

A business entity is defined as the way in which the law of the land recognizes your business. This will differ from country to country and vary to suite different classes of operations. Good business entities (e.g. Limited Liability

Companies) require registration with the government to operate lawfully. In most countries risky entities *"sole trader or partnerships"* also requires governmental permission, however many individual operate without any formal registration.

Even without registration; one will still fall under the law of the land that pertains to *"sole trader or partnerships"* and be exposed to unlimited liability. The following are a few guidelines in selecting the right entity for your business.

- **Qualified and Competent attorney.**
  o Chose an attorney who has years of experience in the particular field (A recent graduate in the legal profession may not have the experience).
  o Most attorneys charge a consultation fee, it is recommended getting 1-3 opinions prior to starting a company. The money spent will effectively guide to a successful business.
  o Do not stay with an attorney who recommends a soles trader or partnership business entity.

- **Certified Accountant.**
  o A good accountant is very familiar with all business entities and will provide pertinent advice for the formation of a company that protects your money and assets.
  o Accountants are also versed in most accounting rules and regulations and can guide to tax strategies which can save millions during the life of the business.
  o An accountant can help you to see monetary systems, accounting structures and efficient profit opportunities.
  o Do not stay with an account who recommends a soles trader or partnership business entity.

- **How to choose?**

- After conferring with these professionals – choose business entities that limit liability and protect assets. (e.g. limited liability company)
- Never chose an entity that exposes you to unlimited liability and increased risk (e.g. sole trader or partnerships).

In conclusion cater for these professional fees as they will enable an excellent start to a million dollar business.

~ The Tools ~

Chapter 7
The Power of Focus
(CS Model)

The writing of this book has taken many years of research and I am generally proud of all the material produced. This chapter pulls on the strings of my heart as it reminds of more difficult times. During my early years I was bombarded by every emotion and thought. This led to positive and sometimes negative consequences, however the processes of getting continual success seems (at that time) unreachable. There were mountain experiences that were exhilarating and valley sadness that seem to shut down the human system. The general successes appeared to generate from the environment rather than a conscious choice.

As the years passed it became apparent that very few people make conscious, value rich and goal oriented driven decision. The general population sways towards letting environmental things dictate how they think, feel and operate. Although good information is widely available, there seems to be a nonchalant approach to focus and strong decision making.

In today's high speed world the trend is toward solving the immediate hindrances. There is little cognizance toward life's goals, enhancing one's existence or creating a mark on society. People look at the speed the world turns and stress about why life is not giving more them. A simplistic quote comes to mind *"life will always test your wings; however it is up to you to FLY"*.

What can be said to hardworking single mother who feel the pressures everyday? She insists life is only about making enough money to feed her family. It is not easy to speak to an emotional or hurting heart. The person is so convinced life will never change, they close their mind to any contradictory direction. The above quote suggests; we are all born with the ability to fly. It depends on us to strengthen our wings, practice the art of flying and take to the air. It is during our flight we see the beauty of creation and our perspective immediately changes.

The purpose the **CS Model** is to provide a "focus tool" for business and personal life. A guide to accomplishing goals and objectives infused with speed, fulfillment and joy. The action of doing this develops quality decision making muscles.

The 3 operating rule I have always adopted are as follows:-

- ✓ **It must be easy to understand**
- ✓ **It must work with little effort**
- ✓ **It must produce results.**

CS Model

> **The CS Model is a mechanism to enable direct focus, enhance intellect and produce immediate direction toward any objective of goal.**

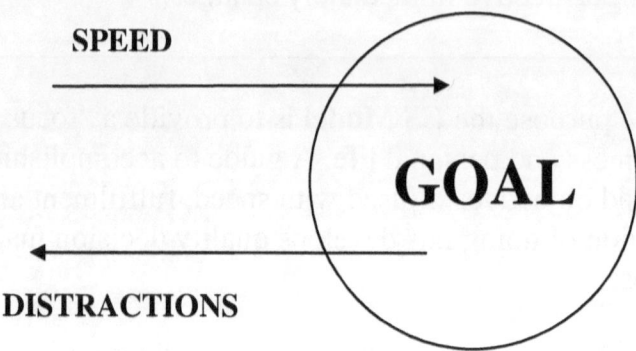

SPEED

GOAL

DISTRACTIONS

Basic Understanding of the CS Model

The CS model is very simple to use, there are 3 areas in the diagram above **Goal, Distractions (Going outwards) and Speed (coming inwards).**

Individuals have goals; it varies from person to person however the idea remains the same. It is defines as a place, ambition, or reality to be achieved. During the attainment of these goals numerous distractions take us away from our aim. Frequent and lengthy distractions dilute objectives and our energy declines. It produces stress which makes us wary and question the purpose of the goal. The stressful state of mind diminishes our ability to think clearly, make great decisions or enjoy the process.

Basic Use of the CS Model

1. Imagine your goal as a picture of large target with one red ring.
2. You get a telephone call that takes you outside of the target, you handle the phone call.
3. In your brain practice to get back to the picture of the target (not your goal) in the fastest possible time. (the key at this stage is speed)

34

4. One you have finish a job or responsibility that takes you out of the target imagine your eyes rushing back to the target

5. **NOTE – At this point do not think about goals – just practice getting your eyes back to the imaginary target as quickly as possible. (the faster the better)**

6. Repeat this target exercise as often as you can, until your brain does it automatically.

7. Fill the inside with anything you want to do.

What will the CS Model accomplish?

If you practice the CS model **exactly** as suggested the following will happen;-

✓ You brain will be less stressed

✓ Your memory will increase

✓ You will immediately gain emotion muscle to focus on any thing you want to do.

✓ Your will notice more things get accomplished as your brain automatically organize all activities according to the CS model. *(The key is to initially practice the model as often as possible until it becomes a reaction of the brain.*

✓ You will notice more time become available to you as more will be accomplished in less time

✓ The CS model can be used for personal and business priorities.

Advanced use of the CS Model?

Reminder; - Make sure you master the basic use of the CS model before attempting the advanced. DO NOT SKIP THE BASIC STEP.*

After completing the basic concepts (about 3 weeks) you may be ready to attempt the advanced use of the CS model. The main reason for graduating to the advanced methods are to create more efficiency, faster brain reactions, stronger decision making skills, stronger visions, relaxation at will and much more.

1. The process is the same as the basic steps – imagine a red target, distractions arrow going out and the speed your eyes returns to the red target after a distraction.
2. At this point you should be able to return to the target faster than a micro second (one thousandth of a second – yeah it that fast!). If not – return to the basic steps!
3. The advance use begins with letting your eye return to the edge of the red target circle quickly. Instead of crashing into the center, picture your self falling slowly and gently onto a huge soft comfortable silk red pillow.
4. Let's repeat: - let your eye reach the edge of the target – then picture your whole body falling gently onto a soft pillow in the center of the target.
5. In your brain practice your self doing slow dives that almost float before hitting that soft pillow, as you body hits the pillow – you let out an imaginary sigh of peace and comfort.
6. Do this step until your eye reaches target's edge in a micro second and you gentle fall is just as quick. (however remains soft and gentle)
7. Do not move from step six unless you begin to experience immediate clarity and comfort at each practice. *(Note :- if the advanced steps is used before the basic it will cause laziness and not efficiency)*
8. Master this advance step for a minimum of 3 weeks. (Nothing less).
9. Replace the pillows with whatever objectives you want to accomplish (keeping the same gentle fall into that goal)

What will the Advanced CS Model accomplish?
✓ You will begin to think with more clarity.
✓ You will enjoy the majority of day – stress free

- ✓ Your memory and decision making skills will combine to produce confidence.
- ✓ You will start to notice a sense of peace with each goal using the CS model.
- ✓ Your brain will begin to move at astronomical speeds.
- ✓ Your thought processes will be hungry for efficiency.
- ✓ Every time you use the advance CS model, your goals will appear enjoyable.
- ✓ Your brain will want to structure and place efficiency in almost all things.

The CS model can also be used to return to your choice of emotion. It will immediately provide a super highway for feelings or state of mind you wish to experience. A classic example of this super chip is the feeling of "peace". If the CS model is applied stringently and exactly as recommended, the effect will be a greater enjoyment in life. A person will develop the emotional muscles to direct any feeling.

Simple replace your goals with the emotion or feeling your want to experience. Follow the basic and advance steps exactly as recommended. It is imperative to follow the rules of use to ensure the greatest benefit from the CS model. The CS model will exponentially increase your power of focus, it is designed to align with the way in the brain works. I challenge you to use this model exactly as prescribed and you will see incredible changes in your life.

Chapter 8
Technology

In today's world every aspect is affected by technology; it produces efficiencies that would be impossible at a human level. Computer chips work faster than we can think and handle several jobs at the same time. In some arenas technology can result in loss of jobs and has forced this 'x' generation to raise their computer aptitude just to make a living. Being computer literate is no longer sufficient, more and more companies are demanding employees be able to handle a wide range of robust systems. An employee who ignores the pace of change will soon find themselves out of a job.

The world's population is now accepting the advantages of e-commerce and email environments. Companies will meet you on your lab top and deliver at the doorstep. The new competitive environment has caused prices to be proconsumer; which is a very good thing.

The dangers of predatory people also arrive quicker to your child's desktop. If not guided properly, some are lured into a pervert's illusion and can be finds themselves in great danger. It is imperative parents embrace the pace of change and competently equip themselves to the tricks and pitfalls technology can produce. The general trend in this new century is towards technological advancement and there is little room for computer illiterate individuals. While this might be a harsh statement, it is much better to be prepared for the 'one' hundred foot wave, rather than being devoured by its immense power.

Technology can be a great asset in the acquisition of your first million; however it is imperative to comprehend its complexities prior to actual use. Brilliant business people suffer from the inability to comprehend and benefit from existing and emerging technologies. It is paramount to any institution to incorporate effective technological systems into day to day business decisions.

On the other end of the spectrum lies the over dependence on technology. On the surface this may appear to be a contradiction; however the ability to distinguish the difference produces financial success. Technology can produce great strides in human efforts but it cannot duplicate human emotion, feelings or aptitude. Every technological system is subjected to the user and should not dominate every decision. Simple put, technology should be a tool for success and not be mistaken as the end all and be all of everything.

It is apparent from our discussion the use of adequate technological processes will catapult monetary efforts into the stratosphere. The key is to find a progressive map that is cost effective and results oriented. A successful company can bear the cost of automation or technological advancement. The man or woman on the street may not initially have that financial capability to implement complex computer systems.

The first thing to understand when approaching technology is to view it as a representation of what can be *"written on paper"*. A common error people make is focusing on the computer ability to crunches, formats or outputs information. They do not see it as a representation of what can be written with a pen. Competence in any computer system depends on the user's ability. A mental image of how the information should look or formulated is the first step. It does not matter the type of system, it is the approach or attitude adopted which produce results.

A pivotal procedure that is by-passed is *"repetition"* of the basics. It is important to repeat basic steps before advancing to more complex systems. If this step is ignored many benefits are over looked and never used. The brain gets frustrated and seldom internalizes or desires to use the system.

The reason is due to the pain/pleasure response – we gravitate to that which we enjoy and away from that which pains. If a particular system is tedious or cumbersome, individuals revert to the manual system of pen and paper.

These two steps may seem elementary however it is the foundation for mastering any computerized system. It also allows internalization of the respective capabilities and applications. The key is not to take short cuts but endeavor to fully comprehend and practice the basic workings before progressing to complexities or advanced uses.

The next question you may have is *"How does this apply to my business or first million?"* The simplest answer hinges on how technology is applied from the inception and during the growth spurts of a business. The following recommendations are not exclusive and you may come up with additional processes to enhance your efforts. It is recommended to implement some or all of the following; this will form an excellent technological foundation. It will also shorten the time and quicken the learning curve towards computerization.

Financial Software

There are hundreds of financial software on the market and each day the number continues to increase. Good financial software may range from $200. USD for basic models and $400. USD for more equipped versions. The manufacturers may differ, however most quality software provides comprehensive financial mechanism. They should be able to collate, track, budget and ultimately gear towards profitability. The following is a short guide to selecting an appropriate system.

Do your research; – If you fail to do enough research on approximately 1-3 version/ models, there is a likelihood you will pay more and get less quality.

Invest in Quality; - After conducting extensive research – spend the money to acquire a quality system, it will pay for it self in the long run.

System Capability - Ensure your system can do the following
o   Track money coming in and going out.
o   Account for assets and liabilities.
o   Employee time and salaries.
o   Produce immediate summation of money available.
o   Can produce weekend, midmonth and month end financials
o   Track budgets in relation to profit goal and expenses.
o   Handle taxation.
o   Produce graphs.
o   Accessed via the internet.
o   Provide adequate security of information
o   Print hard copies for paper records.

Telephone /Communications Systems.
   At the start of your business it may not always be practical or possible to implement a comprehensive phone system. Most quality systems are very costly and require expensive technical assistance to implement. This is an integral part of any business, at this stage it is not suggested new entrepreneurs place this as their first priority. It should be implemented once the business begins to generate sufficient cash flow.
   The work around is very simple, use inexpensive system available for use right now. These forms of communication may be the following
o   Home phone (Land Line)
o   Cell phones.
o   Internet phone
o   Your local post office
o   Local news papers

These communication systems will work well in the absence of more structured processes. It must be remember the computer system does not make the money but excellence in customer service.

Computer Skills

Adequate computer skills are essential in making a person more productive. There exists a misconception that knowing word, spreadsheet or database applications is sufficient. It is important to get proficient at the basic, intermediate and advance levels of any program. The mastering of these programs prior to starting a business will save time and money. These efficiencies can mean the difference between making one dollar or one million.

At the start of a business finances may be limited, visiting an internet café, library or a friend's house can be the temporary bridge. As the business begins to generate adequate cash flow technologies can be purchased.

The ability to tabulate sales in seconds is much better than working figures manually. It may seem trivial however the most valuable thing anyone has is time. The more time available, the less stress and more profit. It might appear to be overwhelming but gathering adequate skills will prove invaluable to financial success. Start teaching yourself today before it is too late.

Chapter 9
Staffing & Training
(CGS Method)

Mavis is manager of a leading organization and in charge a large number of staff; needless to say Mavis stress level was beyond the boiling point. The problem was not staff knowledge. It was how each interpreted the organizational policies. Anarchy brewed just beneath the surface and set the stage for a Montserrat volcano experience. If nothing was done, hot tempered and aggressive individuals would so control the tempo and productivity of the department.

Mavis needed a solution fast or her job could soon be on the line. Mavis took the bull by the horn and faced the problem head on. She took a no nonsense approach and dictated adherence to policies. Staff reaction were compliant, however Mavis could feel the rumbling just below the surface. She pretended to be unaware of the resistance and continued with an aggressive approach. After two weeks of compliance – absenteeism was the order of the day and productivity suffered. The financials reached the board room and Mavis was summoned for an explanation. The company's president was sympathetic to her cause and promised full support until a viable solution was found.

Mavis visited my office and explained her plight. The stress appeared to control the expressions of her face. After a little of consolation, she calmed down. I introduced the CGS Method as a possible solution to the problem. She took the time to understand the mechanics of the system and made a decision to apply it to the staff. Three months later I received a call, Mavis could hardly contain her excitement. The CGS Method had produced and still producing results, staff was happy and productivity was up. Mavis got a promotion doubling her salary.

As a child I always looked at things in completely different way. As I grew up this unique view allowed unorthodox approaches that produced exceptional results. The CGS Model is no different:-

The Problem

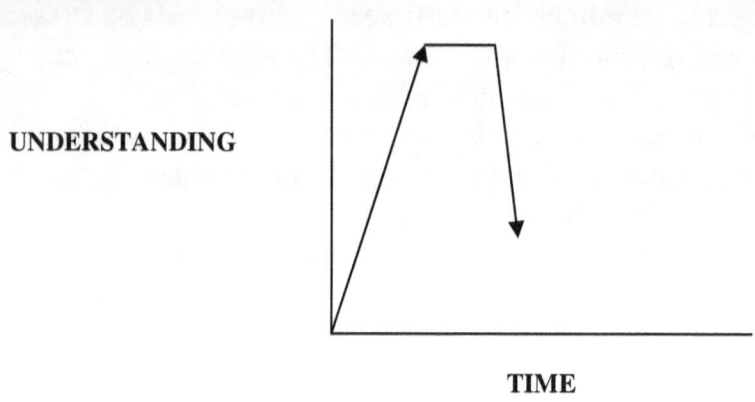

UNDERSTANDING

TIME

The diagram illustrates the common mistake made by most companies. Staff training is done with the expectation that understanding will be the obvious result. Information is received and the understanding of the information temporarily peaks, however as time progresses there is a drastic drop-off in cognizance. This is due to the brain attempting to reduce stress and regain equilibrium. This process causes deletion of any stress related activities. The training is considered *by the brain* as change or new information. In an effort to create efficiencies some steps are reduced, amended or deleted.

The purpose of any training is to bring an individual closer to policies and guidelines of a group or company. The *one shot* training mentality does just that, it shoots information towards a person and anticipates listening, understanding and application. The ability of each individual is vastly different and their memory may be excellent, limited or distracted. The result is stress and the brain's natural goal is always to ensure irritants are minimized.

Another mistake made is the illusion of an excellent or well formatted training session. Great time, effort, intellect and cost are poured into the production and presentation of training. The goal is to make individuals aware of new information of changes in existing policies. Unfortunately our brain does not work well in a stressful environment and often resist the *one shot type training*. The goal of new skills, improved customer service etc is rarely achieved and efficiencies take much longer than expected.

The Answer

After such a detailed explanation of the problem, one might expect the answer to be equally detailed; however it is much simpler than you might think. If the brain always attempt to reduce stress to create equilibrium or peace, training should follow the same principles. Conduct training in a manner that does not cause stress and imitate the way the brain functions.

Step 1- Goals

Ensure the goals are clearly stated, explained and repeated at each training session. The brain works by repetition and the formation of mental pictures. The formation of neural pathways will only take place when there is clear and consistent repetition.

Step2- Involve

After clarifying the goal and training content, allow the participants to be involved in the progress of the training. This causes the brain to question and gauge the definition of the goal and training material. If there is a deficiency the brain will automatically attempt to reduce stress by trying to realign with goal.

Step3- Short sessions.

Conduct training session for shorter times and on a daily basis. A session that is ten to thirty minutes long and

conducted daily will be resisted, however the brain (and subsequently the person) soon become congruent to the session
(not the information). The short daily sessions creates memory, reduces stress and creates skill. It brings new information or changes in existing policies into the forefront of the brain increasing its priorities and urgency. This simple process causes learning, memorization and improvements for the individual or company.

It changes the diagram and corrects the learning of any information:-

UNDERSTANDING

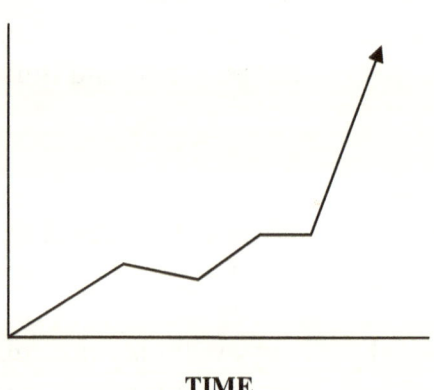

TIME

Basic Mechanics of the CGS Model
Prior to the use to the CGS model Mavis did not realize she was trying to changes the end result and not the core problem. The aggressive approached added to the existing stress and fueled more resistance. The staff found ways of finding equilibrium that were not conducive to the company's policy.
This method of training staff produce results because it works in the manner the brain processes information and memory. The repetition of the goals engages and focuses

the brain. Involvement in the process increases the priority and realigns the body and mind to accomplish the goal/training. Repetition reduces stress and builds pathways in the brain, the more neural pathways, the greater the skill.

I am tempted to go into the scientific explanations supporting this model; however it would not add value and may promote confusion. A technology that is simple and produces more result than conventional thinking is often met with resistance. Test the technology on a group of friends and see the results. Application can then be made to your respective group or company.

The improvement in staff skill and customer service is worth trying an unorthodox approach. The CGS model is another foundation stone for the support of your business and subsequently making more money.

~ *Financials* ~

Chapter 10
Setting up your Accounts
(FCS Cash Model)

We live in a continuously changing world and the pace at which change takes place often outstrip our ability to adjust quickly or competently. The world of finance and specifically monetary models are designed towards sustainability and profitability. They may change in strategy; however the general structure or mechanics seldom changes. It is a common practice for most successful businesses to adhere to those things which make money, and eliminate non-performing spectrum within the organization.

Monetary models may seem a little confusing however once the elementary structure is understood, your brain will soon think in terms of financial models. It is at this point ideas will transform easily into a robust cash cows. The man or woman on the street does not make excess money because they *"think"* in term of income and expenses. Few individuals concentrate on financial models or cash flow systems. The attention is on expense versus paycheck –a mentality of *"not having enough"* is subsequently developed.

The purpose of this chapter is to teach the dissection of any company into their cash flow mechanism. This skill opens the mind to the real value of money and the way it is made. The major challenge faced is the continual battle against historical beliefs developed or inherited from birth. It is difficult for an intelligent person to think outside their comfort zone. It is this "zone" that has protected them for many years. The notion of making a million dollars seems impossible to most and downright heretical to others.

The basic definition of a financial model is: - *Any process or structure that provide a foundation from which consistent and continual profit / cash flow is gained.* Our first step is to develop a fiscal model and guide into personal profitability. As the saying goes *"Being Poor is directly related to poor financial thinking and structures"*. The word "poor" does not mean poverty but refers to anyone who has experienced financial hardships.

The first step is to convert a small salary into a better and more profitable way of life. This suggestion may seem too simplistic in nature; however it was designed to be simple, easy to understand and produce results. Once these recommendations are implemented the following will be experience:-

o *Less Stress*; - The structure will promote the availability of excess cash and subsequently reduce the feeling of not having enough.
o *Better tracking*: - The design of the FCS model is to provide available money and not have to spend excess time tracking money.
o *Financial Growth*; - With a small measure of discipline saving will grow and produce maximum impact on your pockets.

The reason for the creation of this financial model is to provide more money with less effort. They can be applied to both personal and business finances and still produce exceptional result. While there are no guarantees – money invariable produces money, with the right structure wealth will soon become a reality.

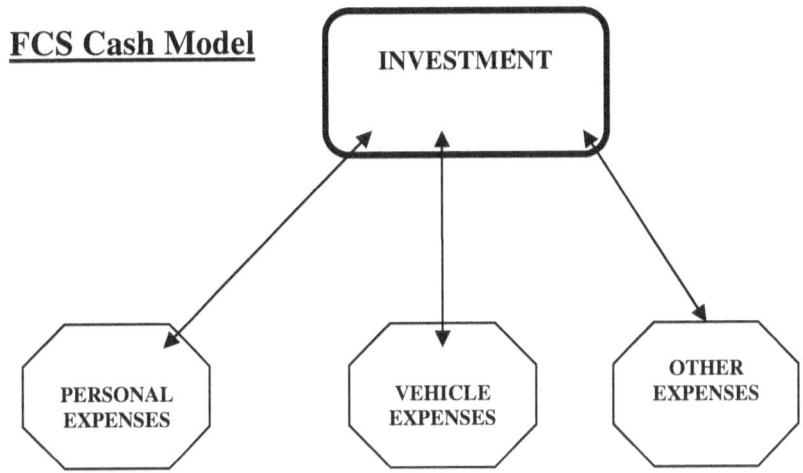

FCS Cash Model

INVESTMENT

PERSONAL
EXPENSES

VEHICLE
EXPENSES

OTHER
EXPENSES

People suffer financially due to the amalgamation of income and expenses. There is only one account for income and the same account is used for spending. This "one account" mentality creates a *"feeling of not having enough"* and makes it increasingly difficult to track personal finances or set the base for wealth.

How to change?

Step 1
Separate all major expenses - open separate accounts for each – keep in mind these are major monthly expenses only and not an account for each expenses.

Step 2
Calculate the total monthly expenses and multiply by 3 or 6 – this will allow three times the month's expenses in each account thus eliminating the feeling of not having enough. (Don't worry about the total; we will get to that later)

Step 3
Decide the most important priority – rank expense account in order of importance.

51

(METHOD 1)- Smaller Salary

*How to accomplish the 3-6 months additional income

- ✓ At the beginning of the month operate as usual, this time credit to the different accounts.
- ✓ The account you placed as priority #1 – deposit an extra $100 - $500. depending on income.
- ✓ Account priority 2 and 3 – deposit an extra $25 - $100. depending on income.

- ✓ What ever monies are spent monthly – replace, however continue depositing extra to your priority # 1 account until 3-6 times the expenses is attained.
- ✓ When the target is reach for the priority # 1 move to the # 2 and 3 accounts respectively.
- ✓ When you have attained the target for all 3 accounts – it is time to move the investment account.

It might take 1-2 years to accomplish these targets, however it is worth the discipline and will set a firm foundation for the growth of your wealth and subsequently the first million.

(METHOD 2) – Larger Salary

*How to accomplish 3-6 months additional income?
Although the first method may take some time – the effectiveness is not diminished. The second method is only applicable for higher income/salary individuals who have excess cash.

This method is based on the premise that large sums of cash can be deposited to accomplish the expense targets for each account. It follows the same structure of prioritizing the most important expense account (#1) - reach the chosen target, then pursuing expenses account #2 and #3 until those target are also met .

The major advantage of depositing larger sums towards the "expense account" targets is the reduction in time. The goal is to provide enough funds for monthly expenses and eliminate the feeling of not having enough. It also enables a base for investment portfolio which leads to making more money.

(METHOD3)- Loans

*How to accomplish 3-6 months additional income?
While this method is a viable means of acquiring income to fund the expense accounts, it is not recommended for the beginner or someone who is already having problems structuring their finances. Without the proper understanding and experience - this will lead to more problems than solutions. (**Do not try this method unless your understand all the risk and benefits**)

The loan method is done via the acquisition of financing from your chosen institution to fund one or all of the account targets simultaneously. It is one of the quickest methods; however the individual must be able to afford the monthly loan installment and also reimburse of his/her expense accounts.

It is imperative to do research first and be aware of the effect on personal finances; this will prevent undue hardship on commitments and family. Once all the details are considered, it becomes much easier to focus on your investments and the million dollars goal.

The Key
Any money that is spent must be reimbursed ensuring an extra one, two, three hundred etc is added to the original balance

Example

Account #1 - $5,000.00 spent - $5,100.00 reimbursed
         $1,000.00 spent - $1,100.00 to $1,500.00

         Reimbursed   A minimum of $100.00 or more
         must be added (Depending on affordability)

This simple measure will ensure that there is growth whenever any monies are utilized.

Financial success or failure is directly linked to the structures or methods by which an individuals or organization manages their money. It invariably will lead to millions in income or increasing debt. The lesson to be mastered from this chapter is to look at financial challenges through structures. It is at this point that old financial habits begin to die and are replaced by cash flow and a cash flow mentality - this is the ultimate purpose of financial structures (FCS Model). Keep reading, you will not be disappointed.

Chapter 11
The Two businesses

It was a dark Friday afternoon and the rain pounded mercilessly against my office window. The radio station reported a tropical depression; flooding and horrendous traffic jams were expected. Motorists who are normally calm and collected may spend an additional three hours trying to get home. This stress also increased the possibility of accidents.

I prepared to leave, gambling in the lottery of "reaching home early or being stuck in traffic". The suitcase was in my hand, draws locked and air-condition switched off, suddenly a loud knock at the front door. The impending traffic prompted me to leave but the professional side did not allow ignorance of the front door.

Resting the briefcase gentle down, I opened the door – dripping wet and shivering was Calvin, a childhood friend I had not seen in ten years. After providing a hot drink and some hand towels, conversation began about greater times and differing views of the political climate.

Twenty minutes later Calvin was calm and warm enough to explain the reason for his visit. It is my business grunted Calvin! What business I asked? My company "Big Movers Rental Ltd", we specialize in providing construction projects with state of the art equipment. The company earns one million monthly however the past two years has been very difficult. I am thinking about closing shop and moving on. Trying not to be insensitive, I enquired what the problem was. Calvin frustratingly explained money is being used to pay expenses and very little is left over.

In an effort to calm his emotions and fry his brain a little, I asked – Calvin what about your next business? Looking at me as if I was mad – he enquired, what are you talking about? You know, the two businesses you are running – everyday these businesses grow or decrease by your direct effort. Calvin finally realized I was trying an old trick to calm him down. Instead of feeding the fire of confusion he forced his brain to become curious about the bizarre question.

Calvin it does not matter the type of company, there are always two businesses running simultaneously. The lack of recognition is due to the frontline business (main operation or activity) unconsciously hiding the secondary business (financials). Business people get so caught up in maintaining the frontline business, they are not aware, or chose to ignore the existence of any other operation. They get caught in an expenses cycle (income invested in expenses to produce income) – a proper interest flow cycle is never realized.

Any business comprises of two businesses – "Main Operations" and the "Financials". The main operation is basically the frontlines operation (sales, customer service, inventory control etc) – it is the generator for money and forms the reputation or goodwill with the public.

The Financial business is the fuel for the generator (Frontline) and directly relates to the proprietor's knowledge. It can be high octane which acts as a catalyst for growth or inferior fuel resulting in expensive maintenance problems. The following diagram illustrates the two business concept:-

YOUR BUSINESS

Business 1 Main operations	Business 2 Financial Operations

Calvin looked a little confused, he explained his accountant tracked his financials, made deposit, suggested investments and produced monthly profit variance report. The company's bank balance is monitored via the internet and we aware of our profitability. A team is in charge of reducing expenses at all levels and report to the director on a daily basis. I am very confused by your suggestions that we are not concentrating on our financial operations.

Calvin was in fact right – his accountant was producing accurate information for business decisions. A vast majority of businesses worldwide are led by this expense cycle. They make money to meet expenses and deduct the surplus as profit. This historic business model worked well in the industrial age, however in this new monetary era it has become obsolete and ineffective. The reason dangers are not seen is because money flows and camouflage problems. The variables that affect production are balanced by money. The more variables that exist, the more money is required to create stability.

If the cost of raw materials increases the compensating factor is an increase the cost of the final product. This creates an expenses cycle hinged on inflationary cost. The suppliers of the raw material also charge more for their product; this creates compounded expenses instead of compounded interest.

In other words Calvin, your business is made up of two separate entities that feed each other in a positive or negative way. The "frontline" rental business is the income producer; this is designed to produce money to keep the business afloat. This is the cycle of your income and expenses, it work once the variables (fuel, part, labor, etc) remain fairly constant.

Calvin, let us pretend it is a rainy Friday and all the equipment are brought into the yard for safety purposes. The yard becomes flooded and a power line falls into the water short-circuiting the two hundred vehicle. What happens to your income? Well I guess the rental business will be wiped out and I will have to come live with you (snickering grin on his face).

This will be the outcome if the two businesses are amalgamated. If the financial operation is treated separately and linked to interest income – the outcome would be completely different. Money should be linked to investments, these should eventually support part or all of the expenses via compounded interest income. **The interest income will never dry up**; it will be paid whether the equipment is rented, breaks down or replaced. The goal of the financial operation is to reach a targeted interest income which can support expenses. If a company waivers from this first goal, an expense cycle is formed instead of an interest flow cycle.

Expenses Cycle

- **Expenses = Income = Expenses = Income**

Interest flow cycle

- **Business = Income   = Interest Income**

- **Investment Balance Increase = Interest Income Increase**

- **Interest Income Increase   = Supports Part or all of Business Expenses**

It is a common practice to concentrate the majority of efforts to keep the business alive. There is little energy left over for the understanding or proper use of financial systems. This business model has become such a disheartening epidemic that a large percentage of talented people fail to reach their financial goals. It originates from historical and cultural beliefs that are very difficult to eradicate. Money subsequently becomes very elusive for the man or woman on the street.

It appeared Calvin began to understand the concepts, however was confused by the mechanics and the reason the technology is not widely utilized. Calvin, an interest flow cycle is the process by which a business eventually becomes financial self contained. This process eliminates the use of cash resources and maximizes the use of compounded interest income. The compounded interest generated is paid consistently. As the balance of the investment portfolio increases so does the interest income. The mechanic of a quality cash flow system is simpler than most people think. It is simple money making money without losing the cash or capital invested. There is no fancy stock purchase or a ten million dollar investment; the interest income cycle is based on consistency and being target oriented.

Calvin, the reasons there is little concentration on the financial side of a business are

- It is hidden from plain site because the business runs on an expenses cycle.
- There exists a misconception that finance is too complex to understand.
- Hardworking business people are too busy and may not realize it is possible to grow their business on interest income.
- The process is too simple and generates fear, doubt and apprehension.

The financial side of any business is so critical; it should a mandatory prerequisite for business people. The lack of skill, knowledge and basic financial techniques cause talented people to propagate and promote expense cycles. The addiction becomes so engrained that people close their minds to any new knowledge. It is not an easy thing to change a person's financial impression of the world nor can we force a change in historical habits. There is one basic rule when it come to teaching financial concepts *"teach those who are willing to learn"* – too much time is wasted trying to train '*pretend scholars*' who don't realize they need financial advice or help.

The understanding and internalization of the two business concepts can be compared to a bridge or connection linking the frontline and the financial businesses. In the absence of these connections a business grows without a proper foundation and eventual implodes. A business can become dependant on production (service or product) and not cash flow from interest income. This unconsciously germinates numerous variables (raw material, overhead, sales etc) for the generation of money. If one variable is impeded there is a direct impact on the flow of money and profits.

An interest flow cycle starts very small and grows by being focused and target oriented. According to the size of their operations a business may decide to support part or all of their expenses via interest income. The way chosen will depend on the proprietor's understanding of financial techniques and strategies. Once a business truly grasp the idea of a quality interest flow cycle, it is almost certain they may never want to make money any other way.

There are many professional people such as lawyers, doctors, and accountants etc who are extremely intelligent. This does status not guarantee wealth. They may earn a very high salary however very few understand or use cash flow systems. The modus operandi is based on aggressively saving to obtain a high bank balance. In most cases the money is held in a low interest account eliminating the possibility of an interest income cycle.

I challenge you to ask your accountant's advice on investments or cash flow. They are excellent at tracking money however their personal finances hardly mimic the vast sums of money paid to track. Being a professional personal does not guarantee great financial intelligence. They are great at being specialist in the chosen field but that is where the buck stops. The challenge remains the same both for the low income earners and the highly paid professional. Historical ideas prevent new knowledge from being absorbed. In some instances status, salary and confidence is sometimes so high, it becomes impossible to impart unorthodox ways of making money.

Human beings are truly creatures of pleasurable habits; they latch onto a singular idea and hold on for dear life. It does not matter if they are drowning financially – the routine remains the same. We have this strange way of thinking - we try the same thing over and over again and (somehow) expect a different result. If you want a different result financially you must do different things to get there. It is not about being a rebel but an informed, educated and forwarding thinking individual willing to accept many ways of achieving a result. We must break free from mental barriers and allow the brain to gain confidence in reaching any goal.

Calvin, a two business mindset or concept does not just happen; it is developed and consciously implemented. The hardest obstacle is the old financial behaviors which fight the brain for dominance. These seek to dictate the understanding of cash flow mechanics. The key is to be focused and target oriented until new neural pathways are formed in the brain. They germinate new routines and habits towards success

At this point Calvin's expression and body language changed – he seem to understand. So Curtis, let me explain what I understand:-

- Calculate Monthly expenses to run the business.
- Place three to six times the expenses in each of my major account (repairs, staff cost etc).
- Treat these accounts like a petty cash system and whatever is used at month end – replaced together with an extra one to five hundred dollars.
- Connect each expense account to an investment portfolio until the interest income is able to support part or all of the expenses
- Continue to build the investment portfolio as high as possible doubling or tripling the interest income.

61

- **Lastly – the only purpose of the business is to build interest income. My wealth is measured in how much interest income generated and not the bank balance.**

The two business concept may appear insignificant to the untrained mind. There may be an illusion proper money cycles exists – "money is made, money deposited in the Bank" – however it is simple an expense cycle camouflaged as cash flow. As discussed earlier, any business dependant on an expense cycle will unconsciously create many variable to produce money, the dangers of losses multiplies exponentially.

Calvin's visit reiterated the financial problems many companies can face. It is very important to overcome historical and habitual understanding of money and move into this two business concept. It then an individual or company will truly realize the power of a quality "interest flow cycle".

Chapter 12
Understanding Business Models

The previous chapter on the "FCS models" introduces basic financial literacy. Organizations may refer to these as systems or strategies, the names may change however the purpose is to produce profit. Companies are so diverse it becomes challenging to understand their financial strengths or weaknesses. This chapter will enhance financial literacy, dissect organization into their financial "models" and produce cash flow systems.

The technique I use to understand any difficult concept is to compare them to objects or things already understood. A simplistic example is to use apples or oranges for addition – e.g. (1 apple plus 2 oranges equal 3 fruits). Make it easy and use any object that is familiar, however ensure it can form a mental picture. It won't be long before your brain begins to think in terms of financial models and the need for apples and oranges will soon be obsolete. During this learning curve it is imperative to keep an open mind and repeat each example until mastery of the concept is achieved.

Frank's Barbeque Stall

Chicken
Secret Sauce + Labor = Product (x Advertising) = Cash Flow
Gas

Frank decided to quit his job and open a barbeque stall, his concept was simple and it worked. He bought chicken, got health permits and developed the secret sauce. Advertising was done by word of mouth, flyers and that incredible smell. Sale poured in; he provided clean surrounding, quick service with a smile and sales increased.

This financial model is not rocket science, it is simple;-

Raw Material + Labor = Profit

The concept can be applied to unlimited branches thus increasing Frank's profit. The major question or weakness of Frank's business is; should he not be able to work the business – would the same quality of product or service continue.

<u>**Betty's Supermarket**</u>

Start Up Money +	Rent Shelves +	Employees Suppliers	= Cash Flow

Cash Flow	X	Advertising	=	Profit

Betty's supermarket is a bit more complex financial strategy than the previous example, however follows the same principles;

Capital + location + employees = cash flow

The second stage of the business model distinguishes cash flow from profits. The main reason for this separation is that Betty's cash flow must progressively increase to cater for Rent, Suppliers and Employees. The point at which Betty exceeds monthly expenses, profit is attained.

Betty sought to reduce expenses by taking stock on consignment (only when goods are sold – then suppliers are paid). A back office administration was created to take care of employee relation, quality control and suppliers. She also bought a computer system that dealt with grocery sales and gave immediate balances of stock in hand.

Betty's only responsibility was authorizing expenses and advertising, needless to say the business boomed. Betty opened six more outlets and raked in the cash. The weakness of Betty's business model is she only focused on income from the outlet, and not investment cash flow from profit. In other words the 5 million in profits is being kept in a checking account to cater for business expenses and not an account that can produce at least a 5% interest rate

$5,000,000.00 x	**5% annual**	**= $25,000.00 monthly income**
$10,000,000.00 x	**5% annual**	**= $50,000.00 monthly income**
$20,000,000.00 x	**5% annual**	**= $100,000.00 monthly income**
$40,000,000.00 x	**5% annual**	**= $200,000.00 monthly income**

If Betty loses an outlet the income will decease and result in other branches paying expenses. Business is therefore based on Cash flow, profit and investments.

ABC Mall & Shopping Plaza Ltd

Bank Loan	**+**	**Consultant Construction**	**=**	**Rental Space**
Rental Space X (Rental Income)	**Advertising**		**=**	**Tenants**

ABC Mall was registered as a Limited Liability Company. A business plan was prepared to a financial institution for the mall's construction. Investors were asked to guarantee the full balance of the construction and the first year's maintenance cost. Investors agreed to be paid returns starting the third year of business allowing ABC Mall to generate income and investment cash flow. A three year lease arrangement was done allowing the first month rental to be waived – this enabled sales for prospective renters.

On the third year – a valuation was done on the Mall's property – it appreciated 40%. The equity was utilized adding ten million to the existing investment portfolio. A monthly sum of fifty thousand dollars was derived at a 5% fixed deposit annual rate. Investors were paid monthly from this portfolio eliminating this expense from ABC's books.

Income from the first and second year was used to start a grocery in ABC Mall's remaining rental space – the space was huge. Inventory was purchased on consignment with an agreement from suppliers to replace any stock over three months old. A minimal profit margin of 35% was charged to generate cash flow. ABC Mall grocery did not have to pay inventory cost enabling very low prices. The influx of customers was enormous and turnover of stock was calculated on a two day cycle. ABC Mall Grocery was making 35% every two days. On the third year of the Mall's existence the grocery was able to match the rental income. It added a further five million to the investment portfolio.

A decision was taken to keep the company a private institution. The success of the first mall sprouted ten additional malls in strategic locations statewide. The major difference is that more space was left for businesses within the mall. These businesses were held to the same rental requirements as normal renters. The difference was they funneled cash directly into ABC Mall's investment portfolio. The only risk or weakness in the Mall's business plan was that a legal department was set up in the second year of business. This could have impeded the growth of the organization in the event of a legal claim.

Hayden Publishing Inc.

		*Self Publishing		
Manuscript Sales	+	*Website	=	**Book**

Book Sales   +   **Printing Equipment**   =
       Publishing Co.

Publishing Co.   +   **Publishing Jobs**   = Multiple
                                                             Income
                                                             Stream

During his childhood Hayden always found writing easy and enjoyable and published his first book in 2001. His research revealed publishing companies retained 75 % of the book's sales and pay him 25%. This did not swallow very easily and a decision was made to form a company and develop a website. Their purpose was to self publish his book. During the first year payments for book sales were only accepted via checks. The following was clearly stated on the website *"Purchases will only be honored upon clearance of checks"*. This safe guarded the income and prevented charge backs due to credit card fraud. It did not mean credit card payments would never be accepted, it was a strategic plan to form a base for cash flow. When sufficient money was earned credit card charge back could be easily handled.

It was brilliant and worked exceedingly well. Hayden attained his first million and placed it in a fixed deposit at a rate of 6% per year. This provided a monthly sum of six thousand dollars in interest income. He purchased high quality printing and binding equipment (via a loan) and allowed his growing interest income portfolio to service his debts. The new equipment eliminated the need for exterior printing and binding services which elevated his income.

When the teething problems were completed and processes were running smoothly, he offered new writers full publishing capability. A rate of 60% was negotiated for Hayden and 40% for the author. This deal meant scores of jobs were coming to the company. Three hundred writers were taken onto the books and two hundred were best sellers. This created multiple income streams and ten million was added to Hayden's investment portfolio.

Hayden hired consultants to translate his books and the 200 best sellers into Spanish, French and Portuguese. The interest income was used to support an aggressive marketing done in the respective countries. Hayden cornered the market and dominated the airways.

Hayden's investment portfolio paid for over ten radio station in each country. Catchy ads suited for that particular culture were played 6 times daily. A large sum of money was spent on advertising. As part of the deal Hayden's company was also given free airtime further exploding the company's exposure. This led to Hayden investment portfolio growing to over one hundred million monthly. The interest generating at 6% was $500,000.00 monthly. The only weakness in the business plan was the speed at which his business grew. In some case, growth must be tempered or aligned with the capability of the organization.

Theme Parks.

Movies	+ Land	= Theme Parks
Theme Parks	+ One Price (All rides)	= Unlimited Park Attendance
Park Attendance	+ Food & Retail Sales	= Continuous Cash Flow

I recently visited Orlando for the first time and was amazed by the beauty, design and wonder filling each and every angle. Every imaginable thing was seen and each street was designed to promote the purchase of food and memorabilia. There was a continuous flow of people; it must have been over five hundred thousand daily. The park operated like clock work, every aspect moved in unison dazzling every eye.

It is amazing how one man looked at an empty piece of land and envisions such an immense undertaking. In our present day this cash flow model goes unnoticed because it so cleverly constructed. The main purpose is to create memories with minimal obstruction or interference from the operation staff. To deconstruct these cash flow models one must understand that theme parks do not sell things. They are designed to create excitement, joy and memories. The result is a catalyst called *"word of mouth advertising"*, the best form of advertising a company can achieve.

The leading theme park starts with a movie that generates cash flow, it is added to an investment pool. The success sprouts a theme park based on the movie. It cements the movie in the brain of the population and lends to retail commodities. This creates a compounded cash flow from the movies, theme park attendance, retails and food.

If five hundred thousand people get hungry and buy an average of $30.00 in food, basically amounting to fifteen million. This figure does not include retail and ticket sales. The culmination of these multifaceted cash flow mechanisms adds millions daily to the investment pool. Investment feed the theme park with its ever increasing interest income. The financial legs of these theme parks are so strong it will make money in a recession or a booming economy. The lesson to be learnt in this example is to generate interest income cycle which grows continuously. Expenses can then be gleaned from the interest income and never affecting the principal investment pool.

Vacation Resorts.

Investors	+	Land	= Resort
Resort	+	Time Share	= Multiple Income

You may have guess that I visited Orlando on vacation and was memorized by the lifestyle, conveniences and unbelievable sites. On the first day of vacation several sales people approached us. They offered an extensive list of free

© Curtis Siewdass 2009

stuff facilitated by leading resorts and hotels in the Florida state. Initially we ignored their advances suspecting they may have been scams. Their persistence peaked interest, we did some research and was invited to take a tour of a five star 1200 acre facility. After the tour, an invitation was made to purchase timeshare for that resort – the offer was great and a deal took place.

During the tour my addiction to the dissection of business models won the focus of my mind. This particular resort refined the art of cash flow cycle systems, interest income and secondary income strategies. The resort is no longer concerned with being fully booked. In fact the only priority is to sell as much time share as possible cementing all profits within the resort.

The developers built the facility appealing to a dream vacation and backed it with a first class facility. The rental income from vacationing families provided the first stage cash flow stream and starting an investment pool. The next strategy employed was time share sales. Simple put - it is an ownership of a week of vacation at their resort or any affiliated resort worldwide.

Time share is a loan plus yearly maintenance cost which secures a dream. Financing from investors was used to build the resort, timeshare offer a loan for each week of the month. In other words 4-5 loans (time share) were now attached to each unit / each week. The resort not only recovered its money, but made 4-5 times profit from these loans.

The secondary income strategy is the maintenance cost. This particular resort has over one hundred thousand timeshare owners. In monetary terms this figure is $87,800,000.00 monthly, however this income stream adds to the investment pool and is never touched. Interest income is used to maintain the resort. It is time to blow your mind a bit:-

Monthly Maintenance	**$87,800,000.00**
Yearly Maintenance	**$1,053,600,000.00**
Monthly interest @ 6%	**$5,268,000.00**

This simple means the resorts income pool grows exponentially and simultaneously elevates the interest income. The above calculation is only maintenance cost paid by timeshare owners and does not include time share loans, food sold at the hotel, rental of rooms or any other income. The main lesson to be learnt is the more refined the interest flow cycle the better and faster the income.

The main purpose of this chapter is to deconstruct business models into their most basic forms. This enables both the novice and seasoned professional to see money in a completely different way.

There are three stages each person goes through after reading these examples – mental awareness, internalization and the reaction stage. Mental awareness is just information your brain accepts as a good idea, however it may or may not be convinced it is valuable for daily use.

Internalization is good ideas moving from being information into valuable and practical things for daily use. The brain constructs neural pathways from which proficiency and efficiency are exercised. At this stage the brain is still trying to get accustom to the mechanics of using the information and will attempt repetition to acquire skill. This skill is not fully developed and is only repetition of a single trend of thought.

The reaction stage represents the culmination of information, skill and creativity. This is where information is fully understood and can easily be used to construct a practical and useful solution to solve business model problems. The brain actually delights in solving these challenges at increasing speeds. It becomes so good at solving problems that every business is quickly dissected into their interest flow cycles. The reaction stage is where

71

interest flow cycles, business strategies and secondary income strategies are understood and used to initiate income and produce profits. The reaction stage enables anyone to quickly tweak a failing cash flow system into an income cycle.

I recommend individuals use these fun models until a basic awareness of the reaction stage is achieved. Practice, practice, practice – it will definitely be a stepping stone in attaining your first million.

Chapter 13
Financial Software

As the tidal wave of globalization races towards us, the right type of financial software is essential for the growth and success of any business. In our chapter relating to technology, financial software was briefly discussed, however we must move from a basic awareness to a more systematic understanding. If you noticed, I did not say complex understanding. The goals of this book are to present valuable information in a practical and understandable format.

While a specific brand of software will not be identified, the attributes of great software would be detailed. Once systems are understood it becomes easier to evaluate and choose quality software. Businesses who exist in the absence of computerized capability often risk theft, human mistakes and losses. While no system is full proof, proper planning can eliminate or significantly reduce these risks.

The two trend of thought to accomplish any tasks are manual and computerized. The manual way employs a great deal of time, effort and cost. These factors contribute to overall productivity of the organization. It limits the speed at which an organization can grow. In today's world it is vital every organization be poised to react to local and global changes.

The systematic / computerized route allows processes technology and systems to accomplish the same task. It generally results in more productivity and less cost. Which would you prefer? Rowing across the Atlantic Ocean or sitting in a fast luxury cruise ship. It might surprise you that approximately 65% of world population chooses the manual ways rather than searching for a more efficient system. They get stuck in routines and never let in a better way. It subsequently affects the quality of life at home and work.

The same thing applies to financial information; the manual approach is tedious and stressful. Financial software is generally easy and in most cases user friendly. The only disadvantage of computerized software is the loss of information caused by a malfunction in computer systems. This can be alleviated by comprehensive data storage and backup policies. Most companies store backup information securely at different location. This will prevent a complete loss of the information should unforeseen accidents happen. In the event of the complete destruction of your system, a paper copy of the data is an excellent backup plan. The key is to plan for failure instead of allowing it to surprise the business or organization.

User Friendly.

When evaluating software, it is very important for it be user friendly. The interface must pleasant to the eyes and easy to differentiate functions. The design should be multicolor and draw your eyes towards the information, however not be so colorful as to create *glance confusion* (i.e. the eyes finds it unpleasant to look at the information). Programmer tends to cram a lot of capabilities into the software, however sometimes ignore the end user. The opens the door for mistakes in record keeping and possible loss of money.

Target Oriented.

The software should be able to track your profit against expenses and provide immediate feedback. This is vitally important to prevent over spending and losses.

Able to provide Financial Statements.

Any program should comply with the accounting standards of your country and be able to provide financials - daily, weekly, monthly, quarterly, semi annual and yearly. Its capability must include profit and loss, balance sheets, tax computation etc – the more financials the better.

Produce Graphical Information.

It is much easy to assess targets, profit or expenses when they are presented in a graphical format. Pertinent financials can be graphed together and significantly reduce the time taken to make qualified decisions. This small feature will definitely reduce your stress and ultimately direct towards continual profitability.

Use what your have.

In the absence of quality software, learn to use the database capabilities on your personal computer. Laptop or desktop computers come equipped with word processing and database base programs. It is wise to learn how to use these programs until cash flow allows for the purchase of a quality financial software.

The lesson to be learnt from this chapter is to find efficient systems to do complex tasks. The reason people make money is they follow a process. It is during the improvement and duplication of the original process cash flow is generated. There exists no difference between you and the wealthy, other than an understanding, mastering and duplication of single or multiple processes. Choose quality financial software and begin to see the dollars roll into your bank account.

Chapter 14
Power of Compounding

One of the greatest gifts to financial circles is the power of compounded interest. It can be described as the mechanics by which millionaires are born and the avenue for infinite cash flow. Compounded interest transforms stagnant money into interest income. Compounded interest is thought to be limited to your bank account, however can easily translate into any investment.

Compounded interest is money earned on existing interest income. As the balance in a particular account increases so does the compounded interest. Financial institutions provide these in varying forms to attract both the low and high income individuals. These financial instruments may be advertised in varying formats however the benefits are similar.

In choosing the right investment there are a few factors to consider before investing your hard earn money. They are interest rate, portfolio mix and prospectus.

Interest Rate

The interest rate on any investment will be closely linked to the level of risk for a particular financial instrument. There is an in unwritten rule in the financial arena, the higher the interest rate the higher the risk however this rule should not be applied globally. There are hundreds, if not thousands of opportunities worldwide that carry a very low risk rate and do provide 10, 30, 50, 100% or more return on investment. The key is to understand their interest flow cycles and duplicate the same process.

Interest Flow Cycle (Portfolio Mix)

The traditional view towards an investment portfolio is to have a well diversified mix of investments. The main purpose is to prevent reduction in the quality or strength of the portfolio should investments perform under target. The interest flow cycle operates from a different frame of reference. It seeks to initiate a small stream of money that slowly feeds itself, until that small stream transforms into a cash flow river. The river carves new directions (tributaries) for the money to flow while continually feeding the river from which it was born. The eventuality is an investment pool that pumps out new business. This enhances / increases the compounded interest.

This interest flow cycle mentality is not limited to a bank account but applies to any business that produces cash flow. The reason main stream investment generates limited cash flow is that it is not linked to a cycle process. If failure takes place at any level, the cash flow dries up and the return for the average investor evaporates. In the following chapters this interest flow cycle will be discussed in greater detail. The present purpose is to create awareness of the greatness of a quality interest flow cycle.

Prospectus

Every single investment is governed by rules, these rules is normally detailed in a prospectus or contract. It is NEVER advisable to enter into any investment unless there is a competent understanding of the investment details. Get accustom to reading the jargon of these documents as it will dictate your rights and liabilities in the event of a disagreement. If necessary refer the "contract" to a qualified person to ensure complete understanding of benefits and risks. Do not sign any document you do not understand or be convinced by salesmen who are only interested in commissions. Do not underestimate or over look the written word, it invariably forms a legally binding document which governs the investment.

Compounded interest (continued)

Investment based on compounded interest is effective due to the multilevel cash flow. The initial principal is invested, interest is added to the original balance – interest is now calculated on your new balance.

Principal investment + Interest   = New Balance

New Balance + Interest   = Compounded Interest

Compounded Interest + New Interest =   Infinite Interest

Although this interest model appears simplistic in nature, it is a very powerful instrument once correctly applied. It took me some time before I understood the magnitude of its power. The following illustrates how I broke down the complexities

My Money + Investment Interest = More Money

More Money + New Interest   = More interest

More Interest + More Interest   = Continuous Cash Flow

I am continually amazed how people work all their lives for income and never choose to focus their attention on interest income. Compounding offers this capability, however the investment must provide monthly or quarterly interest for it to make sense. Annual compounding must offer an attractive interest rate to be applicable.

Become a student of compounded interest, study it daily and soon you will begin to use this tool to elevate the returns in your business and bank account. Ignore compounding interest and you will work for a salary all your life and never reap the benefit of the interest flow cycle. Do you want $3,000.00 salary monthly or $30,000.00 interest income and never have to work for it – you choose.

Chapter 15
Understanding
Interest Flow Cycle & Investments

The purpose of any business is to make money, however the methods for acquiring, growing and keeping the money are vastly different. Some businesses operate only on cash flow derived from sales while others concentrate on investments. These two approaches are not wrong in principle; however do carry hidden limitations. These only become visible when an interest flow cycle is properly understood.

There are thousands of businesses worldwide who develop a false sense of security from their bank balance. The façade of having surplus money often blinds very talented business owners from evaluating the strength of their interest flow systems. It the real world people are only concerned with making money, they are not concerned with having their money work for them. The result is a population whose focus is to gain a pay check, bonus or salary increase. Their whole life is budgeted around the size of the paycheck received and not how that same money can be a catalyst for greater things.

There is no great magic for change; in fact the principles are much simpler that people think. The wealthy has learnt the importance of a well formed interest flow cycle and the great power of compounded interest. Their only focus is to increase the speed of their interest flow cycle. In other words the speed money is invested and reinvested.

While the wealthy have money work for them, they sometimes get latched onto a singular interest flow cycle. This mentality creates invisible cracks in their income strategy. This only become visible when production is stalled or the investments perform under target. Some rich people are not even aware these cracks (dangers) exist. The reason is due to money flowing over bumps in the road and erupts when it is too late.

A business cannot work in the absence of investments, and investments cannot start or survive without a business. It is the invisible connections between the two that eludes some business people. They incorrectly label money making as an interest flow cycle. This is furthest from the truth and why most businesses close their doors. They never master the intricacies of an interest flow cycle.

This chapter is dedicated to the definition and application of true investments and real interest flow cycles. It will attempt to strip away the misconceptions and illusions that exist when trying analyze these instruments. It is vitally important to fully understand these concepts as they will mean the difference between making one dollar or one millions dollars.

What is an investment?

An investment is any mechanism which can produce legal money consistently. These instruments can be a bank account, money market fund, shares in a company or retirement funds etc. These types of investments are considered to be mainstream and are used by a wide spectrum of the population, however there are other investment that tend to generate more return on investment – these are as follows

✓ **Small business** (Localized to a particular town)
✓ **Large Business** (Outlets Nationwide or worldwide)
✓ **Rental** (Apartment, hotels, Conventions centre, Malls)

At the surface these examples may look like a small list, however they encompass any business type or idea that presently exists in today's world. They pick up your garbage, provide groceries, sell new cars and support mechanisms for our daily life and sanity.

These are the literal examples of investments and will form a part of your interest flow cycle. It is very important to understand *investment alone does not make you wealthy. It is the <u>cycle of income</u> not an isolated investment portfolio that generates sufficient cash flow.* This concept blows the roof off most financial gurus because it is based on compounded interest income and not capitalized interest (increase in the price value index* of your investment). We need to move away from the mentality of making investments and work towards attaining our targeted interest income.

An investment or group of investments is only one part and cannot operate in isolation of a properly structured interest flow system. It is a common mistake of to concentrate efforts on making money with very little focus on interest income.

When a business operates in isolation from investments or vice versa – the foundations of cash flow strategies becomes weak and unstable. The weaknesses are invisible and only become apparent when a well structured interest flow cycle is formed.

What is a Business?

A business is any entity that can produce consistent profit legally. There are numerous businesses worldwide which exist to fulfill a need and simultaneously produce profit. They make money to meet production cost and for general operations. The net sum is considered profit and is utilized for business expansion or investments.

Businesses have a power that is unrivaled; this power goes unnoticed and also invisible to the untrained mind. It is the power of *"<u>Multiplication</u>"* – this is the ability to cycle efforts, processes, time and money at incredible speeds. This term may sound silly or unconnected to money making. It is often missed or ignored by the man / woman on the street. This results in a limited understanding of cash flow or wealth building techniques.

An individual might sell 100 items and earn a thousand dollars. A business can churn sales in the millions, generating between ten to one hundred million dollars a year. When this power is combined with a well structured interest flow cycle, income is generated on a consistent basis and growth takes place quickly. Businesses support our way of life and are very familiar. They are not considered to have any particular power with the exception of providing our basic need for food, clothing and shelter.

Our brain is not designed to calculate or track larger amounts of data. As we enter a grocery our brains seldom goes beyond the number of customers seen during one hour of shopping. We do not consider the one thousand customers who were there before us or the two thousand who will be there after we have left. Should each customer spend an average of one hundred dollars on their purchases – due to the power of multiplication – the business has now earned **$300,000.00**. A business which can repeat this compounded cycle ten times per month will now earn **$3,000,000.00** – are you getting the idea?

Which Investment or Businesses are Risky?
I have alluded to the connection between investments and a business, however the purpose of these examples is to *highlight* common mistake made by many business owner and savvy investor :-

Investments Mistakes
The purpose of any investment is produce interest flow; the general population only invests for retirement purposes and not cash flow. The goal of any investment is to build a balance; the monthly interest generated is the ultimate target. It is much easier to calculate your interest to the cent rather than trying to estimate or gamble on the future worth of an investment. It does not matter if an investment is for present or future cash flow, the goal should always be maximization of the interest income.

82

Business Mistakes

There are thousands of businesses worldwide; the general focus is to generate money from sales. This method of generating income is supported by raw material, transportation cost (local & international), staffing and the general health of the economy. In principle this appear to be a very healthy business model, however only when there is a dissection of the cash flow mechanism are the dangers revealed.

- This income is supported by too many variables (raw material, transportation cost, staffing and the economy). If only one of these factors is impeded the business will suffer loss of sales.
- Businesses do not see these factors as a threat to their income because they are widely used by the population.
- Business owners assume sales will continue indefinitely, very important financial decisions are based on projected income. A downturn in sales causes major losses or closure.
- Income is based on a sales cycle
  - production + marketing = sales
  - sales = more production + more marketing
  - No sales = No income

A business based on a sales cycle only will never see the gaping holes in their financial strategy because money is always present. Money covers up mistakes and as mention earlier give a false sense of security. It is vitally important to ensure a business is not based on a sales cycle, or operates in the absence of a well structure interest flow system.

Before proceeding, I recommend re-reading this chapter until internalization of the information occurs as "repetition is the master of skill". While this information may seem complex, it is a base from which all other strategies are formulated. It is worth spending some additional time getting proficient at these concepts.

Chapter 16
Interest Flow Cycle & Investments
Practical Application

In our world there are very few things that cause great change. It is indisputable that without money the development of a country's wealth or status would be impossible. Money is the catalyst for sky scraper and demolitions; it is the barter for salaries and helps individuals qualify for a mortgages. Sadly money is misunderstood, this lack of understanding cause financial pains for many families and businesses.

Money is often the thing we try to attain, "the more the better", however it is never labeled as a commodity. It is the norm to label our groceries, tires or fast food as commodities, however the funds used to barter for these things are only considered as a method of payment. We see our money as the value of our wealth; it is not defined in any other medium or given another characteristic.

Money is the bank balance, investment portfolio and a means for acquiring things – end of story. This is a correct dictionary definition. The mere fact it is defined in this way indirectly creates mental barriers and prevents the proper understanding of money. These barriers generate such apprehension and fear, the world's population never goes beyond working for a salary or trying to save.

Conversely the wealthy have learnt to aggressively protect the true definition of money, to guard against competition and prevent knowledge to the wider population. This miscommunication has different motives, the aim is to define money as something that is very difficult to attain. This concept is so well publicized. It has become ingrained in the population and has transformed into belief and cultural values worldwide. The resulting effect is the population never sees beyond a paycheck, loan or salary advance.

The working class has been convinced of a singular "money" paradigm. They defend their financial status and knowledge cementing the circle of poverty. Whether it is deliberate or accidental, only a small number of people enjoy wealth and know money in its true definition - "as a commodity".

Why use this unusual word? The answer is simple, if money is considered as a commodity, the understanding and use changes. It becomes an item instead of representing a value to be attained. The feeling towards money also changes – no longer is there maternal attachment to the bank balance. It graduates into knowledge and understand setting the foundation for a well formed interest flow cycle. It must be remembered that *"money is a feeling"*, we do not make purchase, save or invest because of money. It is our feeling about money that motivates a decision, not the money itself.

Before entering into this exciting world of investments and interest flow cycle it is imperative the note the following:-

- *Money is a Feeling:* - we spend money because of how we feeling, if there is apprehension or fear, our financial habits and routines are motivated by these negatives. If we seek knowledge and acquire financial skill – spending habits are transformed into behaviors that support wealth.

- *Money should be characterized as a "commodity":-* In order to fully appreciate the use and application of interest flow cycles, it is very important that money be mentally given the characteristic of a commodity. This lets our brain see money as a tradable item. When our mental image is corrected and applied with financial skill, cash flow begins and may continue indefinitely. It is interesting to note commodities (groceries) are traded for money,

86

consumed and the original value of money is lost. When money is traded for interest we receive the benefit and retain the original value of the investment. Interest income is not limited to bank investment, but relative to profit gained from any business or rental income.

- *Money must be connected to an interest flow cycle: -* A business must be attached to an investment portfolio and vice versa. The only purpose of these entities is to produce a singular income stream that cycle at increasing speeds. The faster the cycle, the more cash will flow to produce compounded interest. If these connections are severed or non existent your money remains stagnant. The continual circle of income will never be formed or cemented.

- *Money is not everything: -* Money is a great thing to have, however it is very important to remind you that the quality of your life is not always dependant on money. Happiness, joy, contentment, laughter, fulfillment and the many other jewels of life actually cost nothing. It is there for the taking to those who are willing to improve their mind, heart and spirit. *Never make the mistake that wealth will brings happiness or completeness.*

The Basics
A quality interest flow cycle is an investment account/s that is connected to a business or salary (Employees). One feeds the other until the interest income exceeds the monthly expenses incurred.

Example 1 (Cod Fisheries)

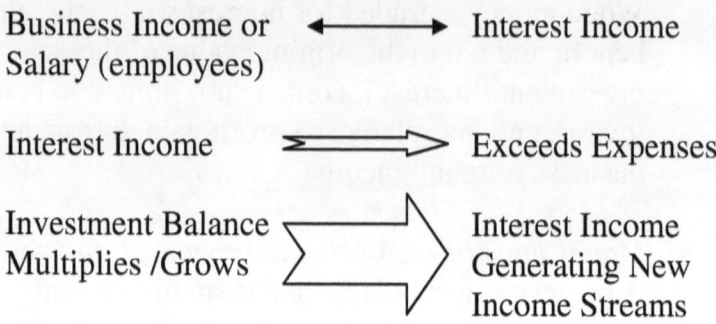

Business Income or   ⟷   Interest Income
Salary (employees)

Interest Income   ⟹   Exceeds Expenses

Investment Balance   ⟹   Interest Income
Multiplies /Grows   Generating New
                       Income Streams

In example one – income generated from a business is placed in a high interest bearing account. The business generates $1,000,000.00 on a monthly basis, the investment account at five percent - generates $5,000.00 monthly interest. Carl and Marvin, the owners of "Cod Fisheries" calculated their monthly expense as $50,000.00. At the present rate of 5% percent – it will take approximately twelve month of investment for the interest income to be on par with business expenses.

During the second year "Cod Fisheries" entire expenses portfolio was being supported by their investment. This business model was used to open fifteen more branches, due to the increasing stream of income – each branch was opened faster than the previous. "Cod Fisheries" took their business globally supporting expenses via a strong cash flow cycle. The goal of "Cod Fisheries" management was to support each branch expenses with multiple income streams. This allowed to company to dominate the market and grow at incredible rates.

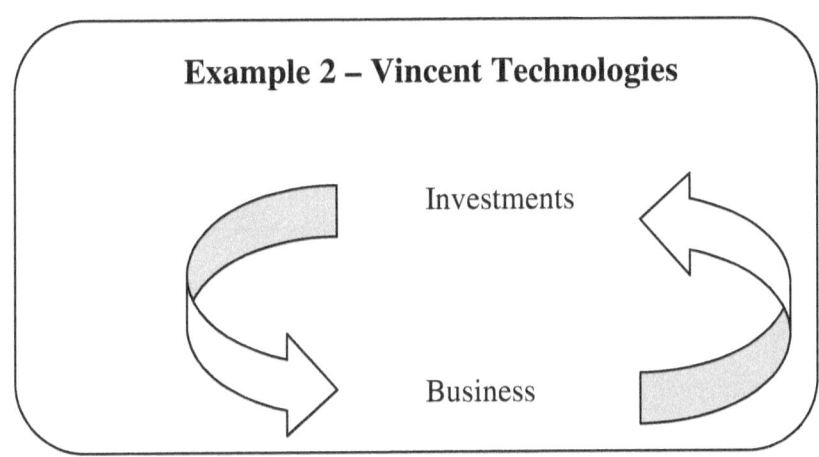

Example 2 – Vincent Technologies

Investments

Business

Vincent Technologies sold laptops, desktops and computer accessories – the company did not manufacture these products, however bought at low prices and sold for over 150% profit. In example 2, the company's aim was to create a cycle of sales and investment. The main goal was to allow the sales to initiate a high interest investment that generated compounded interest. The resulting interest was used to initially buy a small amount of stock. The growth in sales allowed for more interest and subsequently more purchases via interest income. It was not very long before Vincent Technologies investment interest aligned with their expenses.

The second stage was to increase the speed of their cash flow cycle by increasing the speed of their sales. In other words, the quicker the cash flow cycles, the faster the interest income grew. It took approximately eighteen months for Vincent Technologies to reach their targeted interest income, however it was worth the effort as their investment is supported by sales. This allowed all surplus income to generate new income streams and the interest flow cycles enabling growth for Vincent Technologies

Example 3 – Valley Spring Water Ltd.

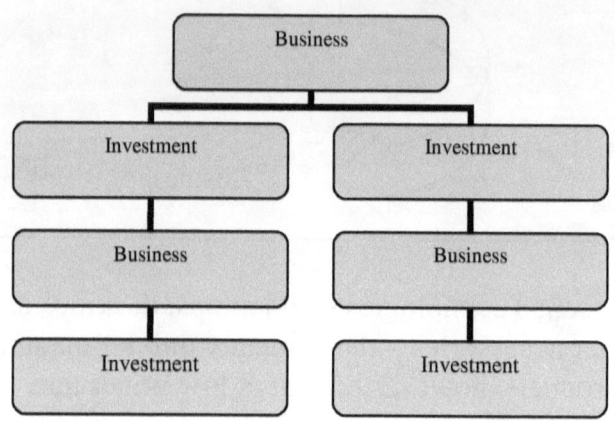

Valley Spring Water Ltd harvest their bottled water from the ten crystal clear springs located on the pristine Valley Spring Estate. The green conscious owner delighted in well manicure lawns and beautiful landscaping. The employees of Valley Spring Water Ltd fondly refers to him as "Mr. Green" and holds him in high regard for his generosity and the size of his heart.

Valley Spring Water Ltd policy for purification is reverse osmosis filtration and UV exposure to kill unwanted bacteria. This decision was taken to maintain the original spring taste of their bottled water; as a result the final product is far superior that the local and international markets. Valley Spring Water Ltd is a small company and do not want to be obliterated by fierce competitors. At a very vocal board meeting the decision was taken to adopt example 3 as their financial model for cash flow and business expansion.

The initial bottled water business was connected to a high interest investment; over a period of two years they were able to exceed all expenses. This achievement allowed for business expenses to be supported via interest income and not sales. The company was never worried about monthly operational cost. Surplus income attained via sales ploughed into the original investments until the interest income was three time the expenses. For ever one dollar in expenses – there was three dollars in interest income.

Valley Spring Water Ltd was overjoyed by the sustainable success achieved and made a decision to expand. All future branches were based on the same cash flow cycle. A business would feed investments and the interest income generated paid monthly expenses. The progression of Valley Spring Water Ltd cash flow structure would read business, investment and then business. One building on the other until ten additional branches were opened and supported by interest income.

The third stage of Valley Spring Water Ltd was to develop a pool of money future branches can borrow from and repay at a rate of 25% plus principal. This meant that any new branches paid (monthly installment + 25% interest); this ensured that the original pool of money would continue to grow and never be depleted. The follow diagram illustrated this concept:-

Loan Model

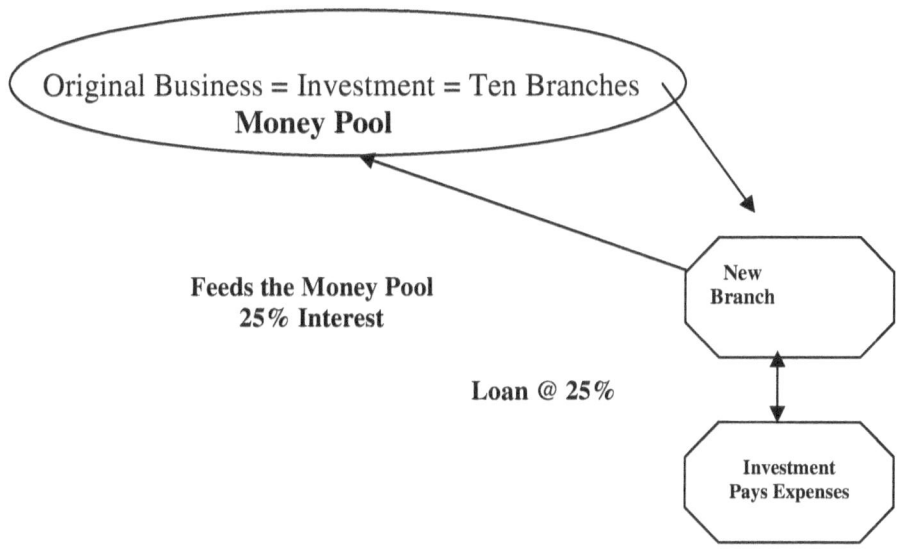

In examples 1 through 3, the different structures of the cash flow cycle are illustrated. Each business develops a cash flow structure best suited for their needs. The main focus was to create a connection from business to investment and allow one to feed the other. This will create strong bonds (interest income, rental income, expansion income) The more bonds created, the stronger the cash flow stream.

In our loan model, which is the advance stage to the cash flow cycle – business expense is support by investment. New branch are treated as a separate entities and must repay the cost to open their doors plus a 25 % interest. In reality the new branch must repay their loan and add surplus income to the money pool increasing the size of the interest income. The money pool became so self contained it replicated new branch at much faster speeds.

It is very important businesses develop a one to three ration (1:3) between expenses and interest income. If the expenses are $10,000.00, the targeted interest income should be $30,000.00 to $60,000.00. This will ensure money will always be available even if there is reduction in sales and problems with production. If an individual or business does not cater for the unexpected circumstances, the expenses will run decisions and not interest income. This creates an expenses cycle and not an interest flow cycle. The business covers operational costs and generates minimal profit. It is very important for a business never to develop an expense cycle.

I am aware that this is a lot to take in; however it is worth the time and effort to develop understanding and master these concepts. A quote I always remember is *"repetition is the mother of skill"*. Endeavor to repeat, repeat, and repeat until the information become crystal clear. This gives you a strong foundation to truly understand money and be on the road to make your first million.

Chapter 17
Offshore Business
& Conversion Advantages

Money is spent everyday to meet needs, satisfy wants and get wasted on desires. Money creates the illusion happiness and can be a catalyst for creations and bad decisions. Money does not produce happiness, it buy comforts which can lead to a sense of joy and contentment.

In the financial circles money is tracked, measured, analyzed and moved around to produce maximum profit. Money is the envy of the poor and a trophy for the rich and famous. It buys expensive yachts and huge mansions, however can be very elusive to the man or woman on the street. The rich seem to be getting richer and the poor getting poorer. The difference is the rich understands the mechanics of money while the poor works for those monetary masters.

An individual of any country makes a living using their own local currency; a dollar represents a dollar and is worth a dollar when purchases are made. Each person is aware different currencies exist; it is seldom seen as an income opportunity. The reason stems from lack of the proper understanding of the country's legislation. A United States (USA) dollar is worth the same to any other American, however in a Caribbean country like Trinidad and Tobago, it is worth six times the amount. In other words, for every one USD dollar, a Trinidadian can get six Trinidad dollars (TTD).

A similar situation exists when a comparison is made between a pound sterling and a Trinidad and Tobago Dollar. One pound sterling is worth eleven Trinidad and Tobago Dollars. A visitor to Trinidad and Tobago who has pound sterling can spend very little and acquire a great amount of merchandise. This is only the tip of the iceberg, if there is a strategy to capitalize on this mechanism, profit will be attained at a much faster rate.

A business that can capitalize on this opportunity will catapult its ability to create a quality cash flow cycle. This cycle is going to be fed by local profits and income from international operations. The pace at which their cash flow cycle become self contained may change from five years to one year. It must be understood each business is different and results may vary, however the commodity we are after is the value of each individual dollar.

Legal Considerations.

Before selling your house, land and car to pursue foreign business or currency, it must be understood each country's legislation is different. The way a business or individual operation must comply with the respective legal obligation.

The best approach is to seek a qualified attorney and accountant for guidance regarding business registration, operations and compliance. This may involve the acquisition the appropriate license and permits which may differ from country to country. It is not advisable to ignore these considerations as they can lead to legal consequence, fines and possible jail time. It does not make any sense to develop these external branches and not comply with the government rules and regulations.

Tax Consideration.

It does not matter where money is made or how fast it is made, according to most governmental tax regimes, income must be declared both for companies and individuals. With this in mind, both a company and individual also have the right to use certain legal mechanism to pay less tax. This may take the form of corporate tax credit, annuities for individual and many other procedures that legally redesign portfolios and allow less tax.

There must **<u>NEVER</u>** be a desire to evade taxes; this not only results in fines and the obvious jail time. But for the working person and companies, it can translate to a garnishee on earned income. This simple means, for every one dollar made, a percentage must be paid to the government until taxes are repaid. The best approach to seek certified and qualified individuals who can guide individuals and companies into the most effective legal tax reduction strategies.

Withholding Tax

Withholding tax is a tax levied on foreign nationals doing business in another country. The rate may range from 5-15% on interest income. While this may appear to be a negative, it all depends on the currency conversion. It is a great advantage to have foreign accounts that are legally registered, gain a higher rate of interest for the same balance.

As advised earlier, it is very important to seek certified individuals in your country and the destination country before embarking on an investment portfolio. An individual whose currency is worth more than the destination country can form a quality interest flow cycle very quickly. The conversation rate may allow rental income, interest income and other portfolio income to feed the cash flow cycle. The effect is a self contained cash flow portfolio. The interest from this self contained pool of funds will quickly generated new businesses and additional sources of income.

Individual will be liable for withholding taxes, in most destination countries they are exempt from personal income taxes. This is only applicable in the country where the person is a citizen. Do the research, seek legal council, be well informed and enjoy this untapped opportunity.

Business Registration

A company registered in it's local country and doing business in another country will pay taxes applicable (sales tax, import or export tax etc) , however may not be liable for the broad spectrum of tax obligations. Although this is an advantage, it sometimes limits the benefit that can be enjoyed should the company be opened and register in the destination country.

In the destination country the company will have to pay the necessary taxes on their earned income, however will be recognized as an entity in the destination country. The advantages are the tax breaks, tax strategies, expansion opportunities etc. This will allow the local cash flow cycle to be fed even quicker than before as there is a direct link to foreign currency. As previously mentioned, seek proper legal and accounting council to ensure your business is properly registered and compliant with that country's requirements.

Conversion Advantages (Continued)

The main reason for the creation an offshore cash-flow cycle is to speed up the growth of your local business and expedite its interest flow capabilities. The main thing to remember is that wealth is not based on your bank balance but interest income. The local business can be compared to a garden hose. It does not matter how fast the water flows it is limited by the volume of water the garden hose is able to carry. An offshore income (conversion rate is greater than the local currency) can be compared to a fire hydrant, the more the stop valve is released the greater the flow of water.

Conversely it can also create an unhealthy addiction to money and germinate the "dangerous" expense cycle. The generation of money that only pays bills. The paid bills produce income and the expense cycle repeats it self. It may appear this model is sufficient, however should the bills not be paid, there is no generation of money. The main premise of every singe chapter in this book is to teach the many "interest income" strategies that ultimately begin a flow of income and what I term as an "interest flow cycle".

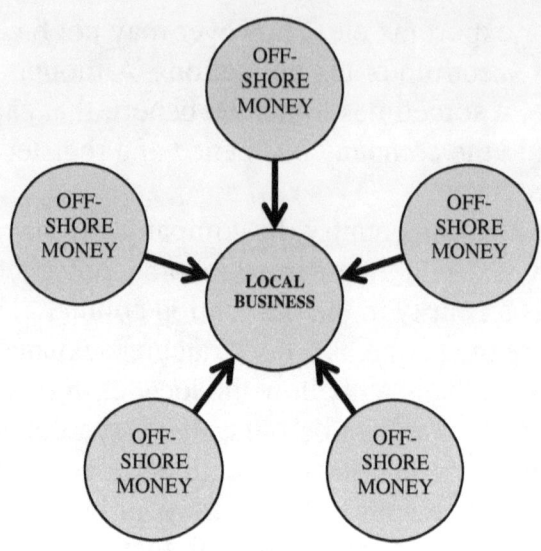

The above model demonstrates an interest flow cycle based on the acquisition of foreign currency. It focuses on the inward flow of money into the local investment portfolio and the creation of increasing pool of money. The main goal of any business is to build the portfolio balance to such an extent the interest income supports part or all of the business expenses. This is the basic definition of a self contained interest flow cycle, the movement of interest income outwards. It requires little influence from outside income sources. The following diagram illustrates this concept:-

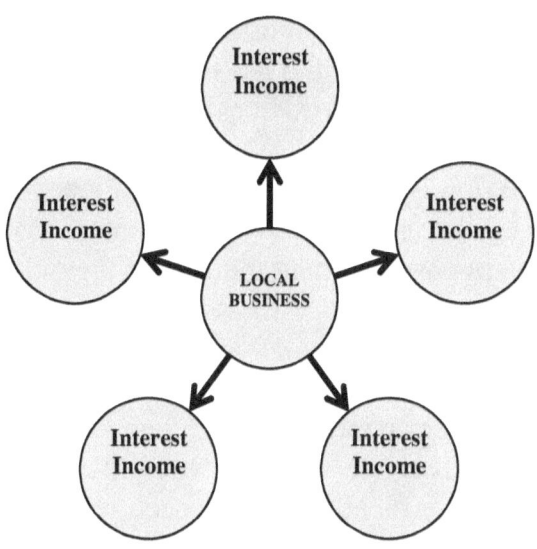

The inflow of foreign currency results in the rapid outflow of interest income. This creates multiple income streams; the pool of money becomes so large it becomes self contained. When interest income generates new businesses supported by their own interest income, the organization becomes less dependant on production. The stability created by interest income changes the historical paradigm on which businesses are run. An organization is no longer fearful of a reduction in sales, as their investment portfolio produces income. The variation in sales become irrelevant and any sales income serves only to increase the interest income. It must not be forgotten the final goal of any investment portfolio is to provide long term income to it owner or owners.

The term "world depression" is being bantering all over the news and seems to be an insatiable catalyst for fear and trepidation. The media has magnified unrealistic realities of the depression; they use words like "loss in sales", "loss of jobs", "financial meltdown" and many other dramatic descriptions.

I want to be realistic, there is going to be loss of job, money, increase in prices and economic slowdown. The world economy will contract, however every person must learn not to be led by fear. World leaders are aware of the financial situation and would not leave their respective countries to suffer. Affirmative action will be taken until stability is achieved.

A depression is only a movement of money from the poor to those who are rich; this movement of money increases the pool of stagnant money for the rich. The historical "expense effect" will soon kick in (making money from expenses). The rich will want to use the money to create more wealth. When this happens wealth begins to expand to the wider population. The rich knows that the more numbers involved, the faster and greater the profit.

The reason for mentioning this occurrence in history is to reiterate the plain fact that a business based on an expenses cycle run the risk of closure. Conversely the business supported partially or completely by interest income together with income streams may survive indefinitely. The essence of this book is not interest income nor is it money. The main journey is the practical application of a quality interest flow cycle. The point at which business profit and there respective investment becomes connected via the cycle of money. The business feeds an investment portfolio to produce interest income. The money generated multiples income streams feeding back to the original portfolio.

The world of currency conversion can be very profitable, however is only useful when connected to a quality cash flow system. It must be guided by a legal foundation and aligned with the appropriate tax consideration of the destination and local country. It is imperative for the respective business to be registered as "limited Liability entity" giving legal protection for their owners. It is at this point the power of currency conversion can be demonstrated and lead to the acquisition of your first million and beyond.

~ *Marketing* ~

Chapter 18
Differences between
Wants & Needs

In the next few chapters we are going to discuss another pivotal aspect of any business, it can be the simplest or most complex. The word we are referring to is "Marketing". Simple put it is a mechanism by which the public is made aware of a product.

Every human being on this planet has mastered "Marketing", from an infant to the oldest person. Each person is a self made marketing professional. Individuals do not realize they have this skill built in from birth. It is masked by worry, fear, trepidation and many other emotional and psychological roadblocks.

At this point, you might be thinking I am utterly crazy for suggesting such a ludicrous notion, however marketing is more prevalent than you think. It exists in almost every human interaction. A baby knows to cry at a certain tone and pitch to immediately attract their parent's attention. It is so convincing the mother or father finds it impossible to ignore the cry. Wives market their needs by exhibiting certain behaviors to gain the attention of their spouse. Husbands are not backward; they have realized by marketing their attitudes, it invokes reactions from their wives. Every colleague, friend or associate also market their ideas by trying to convince others of their opinion.

Marketing is the construction of ideas into a format that convinces others to take a certain action. In this book I have deliberately designed business models, cycles or strategies to be formulated on the foundations of simplicity. The brain has the ability to follow a ten page manual, however all human brains are designed to delete or diminish any stress related activities. As such, over time the brain reduce hundreds of processes into approximately five of the most efficient steps.

The main reason for approaching marketing in this format is to align with the way the brain works.

- It must easy to understand
- Easy to use
- Produce exceptional results.

Some marketing plans are based on a hit or miss strategy, hoping customers will respond to the message. This method is not only costly but time-consuming and can lead to results far below expected targets. It sets the stage for more failure than successes and can de-motivate very talented individuals. Our method is **NOT** the only effective marketing strategy. It is wise to learn the different variations that exist worldwide and practiced by successful companies.

Our method is call "Phased Marketing" and based on generating sales with little or no advertising cost. The creation of phased marketing was borne out of frustration and a need to find an immediate solution that was practical and result oriented. Although its mechanics is based on simplicity, the act of implementation is designed to create discipline, knowledge and most importantly sales. Phased marketing is the culmination of a group of simplistic processes. The understanding and application can be a powerful catalyst for the creation and sustainability of an interest flow cycle.

The following model illustrates the development process:-

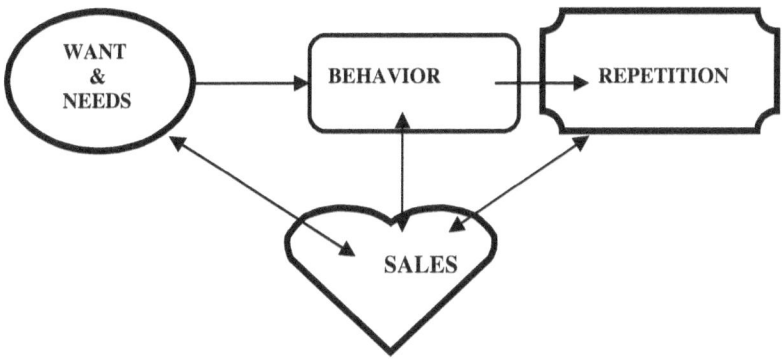

Definition of diagram

The above diagram defines "phased marketing" – it is the process via which a business identifies people's need or want. It is the study of brain's way of processing that need and provide repetition for the message to be memorized. Independently each aspect can produce sale, however it is the attachment of these ideas that generated mega income.

Wants and Needs

In this chapter we are going to concentrate on "wants and needs" and in subsequent chapters discuss the other aspects of the marketing process.

Every human being on the face of this earth desires two things to live. The things they must have to survive referred to as "needs". The luxuries for a comfortable existence defined as their "wants. Age, sex, religion, culture or nationality is irrelevant. Each person in every country will have either a "want" or a "need" or both.

The understanding of these two extremities is pivotal for any business, as it will dictate the profitability and sustainability. It is a common occurrence for talented people to start a business based on their own impression of a good product. It is not based on the actual needs or wants of the population. This results in an expense cycle, the circulation of expenses to produce profit. If the expenses are not paid the profit stops. An improper understanding of "want and needs" causes a business to invest time and resources to fix financial mistakes rather than enjoy profits.

At the surface "wants and needs" appears to be very similar in definition, context and application. It does not seem necessary to spend effort in categorizing these words. The successful comprehension will ultimately dictate the success of any business. A business based on "wants" will operate completely different from one that focuses is on "needs". In fact the product or service offered to public will also be guided by a want or a need.

While customers may have various "wants", it is their needs that are difficult to live without. These needs form the basis for every day living and in some cases survival. If these needs are required by most people on the planet, there will always be a ready market for that product.

What is the difference?

A **"want"** is a luxury item and not necessary for day to day survival. Item such a car, yacht, vacations, expensive shoes etc. These items are good to acquire and enjoy but is not necessary for daily living.

A **"need"** is completely different; they are items used every day and needed for survival. Food, Clothing and shelter are basic needs. A business that chose to provide food can produce cooking oil, rice, flour, toilet paper, soap etc and always have a market for their products. A company manufacturing inexpensive quality clothing will continue to enjoy sales. Shelter is also a basic requirement and the need for it grows exponentially. A business providing homes for rent or sale will always have a flow of income.

Pitfalls

An individual starting a new business makes the mistake of developing products designed for "wants" instead of "needs". They do not consider if it is a "want" –

required for a small section of the world's population or a "need" – a *must have* for survival or daily living.

The question that must be asked before starting a business or producing a product is *"will this business, service or product appeal to the world's population or a select few?"*

If the final product appeals to a small section of people the expandability and income potential will be limited. Should a business focus on products appealing to the world's population, income will hit the stratosphere.

Wants and Needs (continued)

It does not mean a business cannot survive based on "wants". It is much easier to establish a startup business based on the "needs". In this fast paced world the more "needs" you satisfy the greater the income potential.

Human beings are designed to take care of their needs and ensure survival. A business must study these desires and identify the many spectrum of the market. This enables production based on multiple needs rather than a singular desire.

A human being with a need will search the options available until the need is satisfied. If a company provides these options at reasonable prices, excellent quality and great customer service, that company will dominate the market. A good business will make sales. A great business will create an unforgettable experience, and stake a claim in the population's memory. When memory is engaged, advertising transforms into "word of mouth advertising" and become an ever-increasing giant.

If someone gets a cold they are miserable and searches for medication to provide relief. It is the need to feel better that drives the brain to find a solution. The power of needs will direct entire countries to buy more products, services or shelter. A business that can supply their need will always make more money.

The average person on the street is not aware of the immense power of needs. "Good" advertising convinces that satisfaction of needs will result in some form of pleasure. The brain is always attracted to anything that feels good; as such a product addiction develops.

Think about your favorite candy bar, it is not a need nor is it necessary for survival. The feeling achieved when consumed is unforgettable. You routinely search out that candy bar to repeat the feeling. Imagine if this product was a need and required for survival. *Businesses do not sell a product; they sell an experience or a feeling.* If you consider this vital aspect of marketing, it will place your on the road to wealth and financial freedom.

Chapter 19
How people think & behave?

In this chapter we are going to discuss the emotional bridges which attract people to your product. It is vital to understand the brain's decision making process, its use in marketing. A keen knowledge of how people think and behave will increase sales and the ability to dominate the market. If a business ignores the *'humanity of sales'* they will not capture valuable niches.

Since the rise the mighty internet gauging behavior has become increasingly difficult. Most businesses have gone global (via the internet) and forced to radically change perspectives toward sales. "Customers" sit behind their computer, in the privacy of their own home and make purchases. The identification of the customer becomes impossible and new methods must be developed for progress.

The identification of sales patterns is no longer easy or clearly visible. A business can no longer sort customers by ethnicity, age or gender. In this technologically advance times, it is impossible to tell who is actually making purchases. This "hidden" factor has caused many expensive marketing errors.

The derelicts of failed marketing program are evident by lackluster profit and closure of some entities. What then is the key to look beyond the façade of the "hidden" customers? It is found in the *"humanity" of sales*.

Every human being on this earth is designed for survival. While some may be more successful than others, the goal is to ensure survival is priority number one. This instinctive desire is the reason *"humanity" of sales* becomes most applicable.

This abstract description seems irrelevant; however the understanding of humanity polishes and hones many marketing and sales concepts. It is not a grand marketing scheme but the thing which makes people feel good about themselves and others.

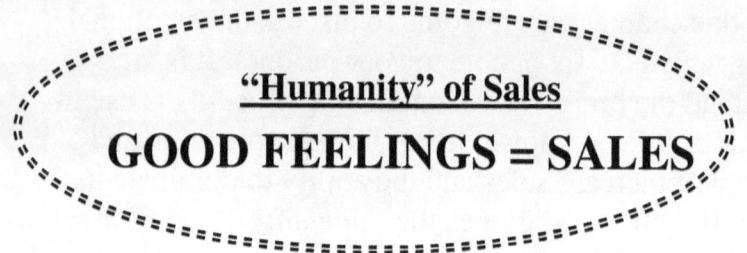

George & the Gift Store

George worked for minimal salary at the plastic company and never viewed life as lacking any thing. He made a decision to healthfully enjoy every minute's life offered. It was wonderful day and he decided to visit his favorite gift shop located minutes from his office. They sold top quality colognes, it made him smell nice, feel good and more confident to be around people.

The gift store was clever and knew this cologne was a top seller. They placed a sign in plain view of the men's cologne "Make your wife feel special buy……..". The sign had a picture of a woman in ecstasy receiving the female version of the cologne. At the female section, the sign read "Make the man in your life feel special buy…." It was not long before that brand of cologne was sold out.

Lesson 1

SELL A FEELING OR EXPERIENCE NOT A PRODUCT

Marketing and sales is about selling a feeling or experience, it is not about selling your product. The product may satisfy a particular need but it is the feeling or experience that keeps them coming back for more.

A product marketed by it characteristic only will produce limited sales. A product should highlight the feeling or experience. The sales generated will start the memory process and word of mouth advertising. This goal of any marketing plan is to be implanted in the memories of the population and grow via "word of mouth advertising".

Lesson 2
IGNITE THE IMAGINATION

Sales and marketing are hinged on the business ability to "ignite customers' imaginations". If a marketing plan appeals to feelings and experiences of the audience, sales will automatically follow.

Have you ever seen an effective travel/vacation advertisement? The ad shows peaceful images of families having fun, laughing and enjoying each other's company. It also highlights the attributes of the five star hotels. The pictures or images ignite the imagination of an onlooker. This births a seed of desire replaying continually in the brain. It is this simplistic occurrence that results in the purchase of a ticket.

Lesson 3
TELL THE TRUTH

In the business world, (unless dictated by law) morality and ethics sometimes go out the window. Instead of insisting on the truth about a product, some companies overlook flaws or limitation for short term profit. There is an unsaid modus operandi among some electronic companies, where parts and components of a product are designed to last a very short time. The person who purchases a product will only have usage for a limited time.

In the world of business, the reputation of your product spreads very fast to the local and international population. If there are any flaws or untruths, it will be recognized by the man and women on the street and high powered professionals. It is not wise to mislead a population, negative "word of mouth advertising" will break down the façade of a company and sales will plummet.

It is possible to generate sales with the use of these 3 principles; however the complete application of "phased marketing" will be cover in a later chapter. At this stage it is important to internalize these 3 lessons. It is designed to germinate foundational understanding of marketing and the things that generate sales.

"Humanity" of Sales continued

The reason for the development of phased marketing is to bridge the gap for the beginner and introduce a fresh perspective for season marketing professional. I have always strived for the best, but understanding focused human beings will improve their situation. As such better ideas may be discovered. "Phased marketing" taught in this book should be influenced by any new discoveries and trends.

This basic focus of this chapter is "how people think and behave" and the "humanity" of sales. The understanding of thoughts and behaviors produces great results. Marketing is not only fact and figures on a report; each sale that contributes to a bank balance represents a human being. The "humanity of sales can be summarized as follows:-

HUMAN BEINGS x TIME = MEMORY

The learning curve of everything human is carved by the passage of time and produces good or bad thoughts. The resulting behavior will define the individual, what they do and the person they represent.

The humanity of sales must be based on the understanding of this concept. It is the human being who makes the purchase not a sales report. A human being will spend money to satisfy a need. They spend more money for products that gives quality, guarantees, honest (does exactly what the advertising claims) and makes them feel good.

The above equation is not based on tracking age, gender or ethnicity. The foundational principle is to see human being as human beings. A marketing plan must encompass the ideals of human being and time to produce memory. A purchase is made based on an individual "remembering" a product and seeking it out.

MEMORY x REPETITION =   THOUGHTS & BEHAVIOURS

It is not recommended you memorize these formulas. The concepts are to provide foundational understanding of marketing and the human effect. Human beings have a great desire and affinity to communicate professionally, personally and at a cultural level. It is can be referred to as an "unstoppable addiction" crossing gender, age and cultural barriers. If something happens in a remote village, it isn't long before the entire country becomes aware of that particular occurrence. Human beings love to tell "what has happened" or "what is going on" – this is the way the knowledge is acquired-the voluntary or involuntary exchange of information.

BEHAVIOUR = WORD OF MOUTH = SALES

Word of mouth advertising is the ultimate goal of any business. Since the rise of the internet, "word of mouth advertising" takes place ten times faster. It is a valuable tool for developing a self sufficient marketing program. The business becomes so well known, very little effort is needed to maximize sales.

Successful marketing plans are focused on solving problems which make people feel good. When people feel good about a business, website or product they make more purchases. It is the cumulative purchases coupled with an "interest flow cycle" that produces more income.

As we conclude this chapter you must have a basic understanding of human thoughts, behavior, humanity of sales, formulas (human being to sales) and the addiction to spreading information. If these are unclear and appear "fuzzy", it is recommended you revisit the concepts. It would not be long before you master them and attain more money.

Chapter 20
Branding

What is branding? Maybe it has something to do with cattle ranching. You know, the mark seared onto an unlucky cow's hide to identify the owner. It might have something to do with shoes, young people these days are always looking for the latest brand name shoes to puff up their reputation. Alcohol! The thing served in most bars worldwide.

It might sound like a very confusing word, however in the context of marketing – branding is a very important aspect of all businesses. Any product that is produced by any business has a singular purpose – Branding. The understanding of this word eludes a majority of small business owner and even some establish businesses. The reason is the same all over the world, people concentrate on making money. There is no priority for the development of a quality interest flow cycle or a self contained marketing system (sales flow cycle – interest income supporting sales expenses)

The basic definition of branding is the conversion of an unknown product into a house hold name. Branding is the point at which the population fondly swears by use of a product. The reason is due to the trust developed between the business, brand and respective customer base. Simply put, branding is transforming something that is unknown into a clearly recognized product. The sole purpose is to generate memory and sales.

The concept of phased marketing includes branding however presented in a different way. Sales are hinged to the local and international population knowing and repeating the name of the product. This is why branding is so important and meticulously studied.

Francis Pure Honey

Francis loved flowers; he grew a wide variety of exotic varieties. It soon grew into a three large botanical paradise. Strangely enough, he did not sell his exotic plants, he just loved his hobby.

Francis visited a nearby honey farm and fell in love with the business of producing honey. Needless to say, it was not long before he started his own business which grew into two hundred individual nest or hives. "Francis farms" produced the highest quality honey in the region and marketed as "Francis farms pure honey".

A clever individual and a strewed business man, Francis utilized phased marketing to generate a name for the farm and a brand for his product. The name grew so well it appeared on the shelves of every supermarket and was cemented in the memory of the population.

Francis registered the name "Francis farms pure honey" as a trade mark for his brand of honey. He consulted his attorney and accountant to enable an accurate legal foundation for his product, its name and the way in which the brand was recognized. The top local import/export brokers were also contacted providing the necessary requirement and legalities for international export.

The internet was utilized to source customers, international sales grew slowly however was consistent. The brand "Francis farms pure honey" soon appears on all major internet mediums. Income from sales was utilized to form a "sales flow cycle" – interest income supporting all the advertising expenses. Francis only focus was to increase his portfolio balance and consequently interest income. Needless to say, Francis made a whole lot of money and was a very happy camper indeed.

BRANDING = PROPER LEGAL FOUNDATION

Branding a product is a very easy process, however the legal foundation required to keep competitors at bay is a little more difficult. This book is not dedicated to "trade mark" ™ or "registered" ®, however the reason for mentioning them is to provide a basic awareness of their existence.

Most people are oblivious to the symbols ™ and ®, however if you look at any international product; these symbols are visible albeit very small. The symbol ™ and the insignia ® declares to the world that a particular product has been legally registered and now have specific intellectual property rights. A business granted permission to use these symbols can protect themselves from any unauthorized use of their business name, product or related slogan. This is vitally important if a product is sold globally, there are many unscrupulous individual eagerly waiting to capitalize of your efforts.

BRANDING = MEMORY

Effective advertisements utilize memory. It may appear this is automatic; however there is a science behind the memory process. The brain continually absorbs information, however is activated by specific triggers. Our memory is based on the following

Movement – Advertisement utilize lots of movement, usually disguised as humor, dance or strange effects. Successful businesses seek eccentric movements, this serves to cement memory in the brains of the potential customer.

Color – The brain remembers things in color, the more vivid the spectrum the more likelihood memory will be engaged. Colors are either sprinkled as a backdrop to the main product or an aggressive focal point highlighting attributes. Memory is not only engaged by color but recalls in color. We do not remember an event in black and white, we remember in color.

Pictures – Memory is a series of pictures, it is not words. Even if words are part of the memory, the brain stores information as a series of pictures. Think about a lion, do you recall the word lion or a picture of a lion? A picture of a lion automatically jumps into your mind. Most effective advertisement is based on these three principles – movement, color and pictures. Once these are exaggerated, memory becomes automatic and the branding process begins.

BRANDING = REPETITION

Once there is a proper legal foundation and the memory is engaged, the next stage to branding is repetition. The more an advertisement is repeated, the better the chance for it to be remembered by a potential customer.

As previously mentioned, this chapter is not designed to give a comprehensive guide on branding, the purpose is to allow awareness and make preparation to fully understanding "phased marketing". This is definitely another step towards making more money.

Chapter 21
Statistic vs. Results

During my high school years I hated mathematic and frankly did not see its use or application. How would algebra or simultaneous equations be applied to daily living? , it just did not make any sense. Needless to say, my grades were not scholarship material and there was no motivation to learn.

It was not until my later years I developed an affinity for mathematic and statistics. The "joy" of statistics started when I figured out how to create a database to calculate interest income. Spreadsheet was done for my bank balance and projection made for ten, twenty, thirty, forty years. Amendments were made to the interest rate and calculation done for all interest due. The monthly saving was varied and the impact on retirement income was clearly seen. Anything thing that could have been changed was changed. The resulting effect was a comprehensive understanding of money and its mechanics.

As you probably guess by now, it soon grew into an insatiable desire to break down, dissect, reconstruct and manipulate business models and techniques. It has become so reactive my brain automatically races towards the monetary construct of any business and investment. It is an amazing thing to understand how money affects the everyday individual, small businesses and the multimillion dollar enterprise.

It might be misconstrued these three monetary spectrums do different thing to attain their profit. The truth is they operate from different angles of mathematics and statistics. The money making techniques may be very similar albeit at larger scales. It is the manner in which money is measures, tracked and calculated that makes the difference.

The strength of any business is directly related to the management's ability to fully comprehend financial statistics. Reference is not being made to advance calculations but to the common sense ability to calculate profit – income less expenses. This basic calculation is the goal of the any business, the variation of income or expenses to produce more profits.

Why is statistics necessary?

Profit means absolutely nothing if the recipient lacks the ability to manipulate data. The day to day operation of any business produces fact and figures. They are used to form a statistical picture of financial, marketing or human resources. The collection of financial information is used to generate daily, weekly, monthly and yearly accounting reports. Sales data is utilized to analyze the effectiveness of a particular marketing strategy. If a business does not keep statistics on employee attendance, then absenteeism will affect business operations.

Without the use of statistics, it becomes impossible to make profit on a long term basis. Decision making will becomes arduous and the motivation to keep the business will be eroded. The recognition of problems becomes difficult. Money camouflages many dangerous financial and marketing errors. The risk is not only the closure of the entity, but impending litigation.

People unknowingly use statistics every singles day of their lives. They estimate expenses, make monthly budgets, calculate gas consumption and use data to choose the most efficient route for every trip. When we take vacation, research is done to ascertain the most cost effective travel agent with the best reputation. In the event a mortgage, data is utilized by the mortgagee to calculate a monthly installment. If we go to the gym, statistic is used to time each workout and the growth in the fitness level. We use statistics to cement our love life, during a date the attributes of the person is dissected to form an emotional picture of their honesty and intention.

Whether you are willing to admit it or not, statistics forms part of our daily lives. The brain operates by creating a database of memories from which decisions are made. It will attempt to remove or suppress unpleasant memories and move us away those situations. These are a few examples of the presence, frequency and the power of statistic.

The difference between a dollar and a million dollars is basically an ability to use raw data to calculate monetary gains. The old adage becomes true "you do not need money to make money". The only skill required is mastering the ways profit can calculated. There may not be a dime in your bank account, however if you can learn monetary mathematic (profit calculation) and statistics (crunching raw data), money will flow freely. A CEO who earns millions per years has learnt a basic skill – the ability to use statistics to gauge profitability or impending losses. He is also able to use variances in data to create financial solutions keeping profits to a maximum.

The Simple Approach

Before you throw in the towel and run in fear of facing these complexities, it is recommended you take an about turn and appreciate its simplicities. Statistic is very simple and need not to be feared. The only challenging thing is the use of a computer to do the work. Computers in today's world are user friendly and the understanding of "formula" and database manipulation has become easy. If you are lacking in the computer skills, there is a vast amount of information available on the internet.

This chapter is not about advance mathematical equations or complex statistical variations. The purpose is to format the use of mathematics and statistic in a manner in which anyone can understand. There will be no reference to complex ideologies that can confuse the understanding of these principles. There are three element used in the simplification of raw data:-

121

✓ **List => Calculate => Monitor.**

Listing Data

The most important skill to learn is listing data in a format which is understandable. There is a misconception that listing raw data is a natural process and requires very little common sense, however the opposite is true.

Many business people mistake hard work for progress. They have the ability to count money however do not know how to list its monetary construct. The monetary mechanics that produces their income are almost invisible.

An understanding of the "commodity of money" is nonexistent. A fatal flaw of talented employees and business people is getting caught up in an expense cycle. This robs them of the ability to see monetary dangers which can ruin families and businesses.

The correct listing of data can lead an interest income cycle. The incorrect listing of data leads to the most dangerous financial situation – an expenses cycle. Data should lead to a conclusion and not to confusion or stress.

A computer system is an important tool in the crunching of data however the database must not contain irrelevant information. A concerted effort should be made to ensure the data being tracked is relevant to the reporting process. With this in mind, choose wisely data being listed, calculated and monitored. The computer software or system is just that, "a computer system" – it will only process information provided. In other words "garbage in – garbage out", a computer is controlled by the human and not the other way around. A mistake in the reporting process "in most cases" is due human error and not the computerized system.

Calculate (Using Formulas)

Most spreadsheet applications enable addition or subtraction via the use of formulas. These are very useful

122

for the automatic summation of a group of data or just two variables. It is also possible to link figures in different spreadsheet to produce a specific report.

The versatility of spreadsheet formula is amazing, it is bit challenging to understand but worth the effort. When one becomes proficient, business operations can be assimilated by the use of spreadsheet and relevant formulas to link different databases. The reporting process only takes a few clicks and required reports or queries are quickly obtained.

Monitor

The monitoring of final reports is the life blood of any organization. The best way to do this efficiently is by the graphical representation of data. When compared to tabular reports, decision making is faster if the upward or downwards trends can be seen. A graph showing profit targets compared to actual sales will gives decision makers a pictorial image of these ratios. This image will be utilized to make minor or major changes to strategies and maximizes profits.

Purchase Software.

It is an asset to learn the above, however the purchase of readymade software allows for the seamless tracking of payments, deposit and profit. It is important to ensure the software has multiple capabilities to track financials, marketing, human resources, taxation and assets. This will bridge the computer literacy gap and allow business operations rather than being overwhelmed by record keeping.

Statistic vs. Results

In preparation for the chapter on "Phased Marketing" it is important to use statistics to guide effectiveness and profitability. In the absence of financials, money is wasted and a dangerous "expense cycle" begins to develop (money camouflaging mistakes).

NUMBER OF SALES = EFFECTIVNESS OF MARKETING

The number of sales will determine the effectiveness and profitability of any marketing strategy. If important to keep data on each marketing plan, this will enable accurate reporting and subsequently changes in strategy.

PLAN A	50 SALES
PLAN B	20 SALES
PLAN C	200 SALES

It is clear from the above data that plan C appears to be the most effective marketing plan. The accuracy of records and the testing of each plan and must be top priority. Without a sales report, the decision to increase funding in plan C will be very difficult.

TESTING = CHANGE = MORE SALES

The use of statistical data allows for testing, change in strategy and subsequently more sales. Start with a small advertising budget, test and make changes to the marketing message, look and product profile. Without the development of an accurate database, these decisions are impossible and expensive.

Conclusion

It is impossible to list all the application of Statistic vs. Results; however the importance of accurate record keeping is paramount to your success. A comfortable level of proficiency in the use of spreadsheet application or readymade software should also be top priority.

The difference between the successful person and the unsuccessful is their knowledge and skill. This can only be acquired via an open mind and a willingness to learn. I have never agreed with the old adage of *"working hard to get results"*, my main goal has always been *"working smart"* to achieve knowledge, skill and proficiency. The achievement of these tools creates the foundation for creatively and ultimately success.

Chapter 22
Phased Marketing

After so much preparation the time has finally come to explore the greatness of ***"Phased Marketing"***. During our journey we have discovered the differences between wants and needs and the manner in which people behave. There were discussions on memory and its subsequent use in the process of branding. Simplistic method to track effectiveness and efficiencies concluded the foundational stages.

It is fitting to provide some background for the creation of *"Phased Marketing"*. During my early years money was scarce and I was asked to assist in selling vegetables "door to door". Our neighbors had numerous questions before they bought and this frustrated my little five year old brain. I could not understand the problem nor increase sales. I quickly observed the more vocal the sales pitch, the easier money was earned. The more aggressive the approached, the quicker prospective buyers became attentive and tuned into the sale. This become catalyst to find a simplistic way to make sales and so was born *"Phased Marketing"*.

What is Phased Marketing?

As the name suggest, it is a phased process to market any product. The difference from main stream is that Phased Marketing is designed for everyday people. The phased process begins with the use of free marketing methods and culminates with comprehensive media coverage.

The Golden Rule!

The goal of phased marketing is to generate sufficient sales to produce interest income. This income will be use to support part or all of the monthly advertising costs. In other words, monthly interest income derived from an investment

126

portfolio is consistent and can be accurately calculated. The net effect is that 100% of the principal sales income is retained while advertising budget (interest income only) continues to grow on a monthly basis. This creates a cycles system or a flow system that I have termed as *"Sale Flow Cycle"* - *the continual generation of interest income to support all marketing efforts.*

The only goal of any business is to invest and invest until interest income is sufficient to support marketing strategies. This must be top priority and take center stage at each and every meeting. The reason for its importance is to hinged sales and marketing with the glue of interest income. A cycle of money is formed; this money will be there even if sales decline. While other companies exhaust their principal income and saving, your organization may never run out of money to promote products. This is the power of a quality *"Sale Flow Cycle"* - using money to create money and not necessarily the efforts of sales. While sales will initially form your startup income, it is imperative the focus immediately be switched to the attainment of targeted interest income.

As mentioned in the chapter on "The two Businesses", organizations focus on the activity of the making money. This is called the frontline business, the generator of the money or the monetary mechanics for profit. They seldom realize the importance or the urgency of mastering the financial or monetary side of the business. The real power of interest income is overlooked, never used and eventually become obsolete. The end effect is that large sums of money are left in low interest accounts. It produces no recurring benefits (interest income) – once the principal is utilized no further considerations can be made.

"The Golden Rule" remains the same, make a concerted effort to realign your business to produce interest income from day one. Start small and build habitual momentum, it would not be long before the targeted interest income is achieved. Do not stray from this rule. The stress of the day to day operations will attempt to pull your attention away from the interest income goal. Guard your mind and priorities closely and ensure the *"Sale Flow Cycle"* is achieved above other business goals.

Phased Marketing (Structure).

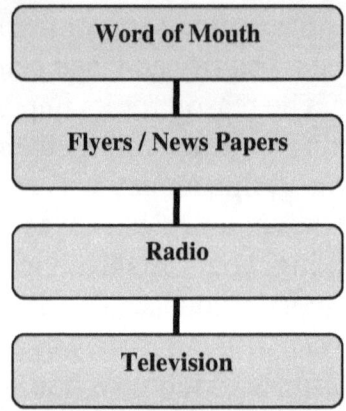

Word of Mouth.

The cheapest form of advertising is "word of mouth"; it cost nothing and is completely free. "Word of Mouth" is simple telling people about your product. It involves calling associates, coworkers, friend and family member to advertise a product. It is a very personal way of spreading the word, for some individuals it is very enjoyable while others shun this method.

This may sound like "the run of the mill" advertising however there is a science behind the madness. Phased marketing is based on producing progressive sales via a staged process. Movement is only made when a targeted number of sales are achieved and the ability of the income allows for progress. There is never any growth unless sales are realized. In this way the business supports it self and does not become a financial burden to the business owner.

The humorous side of this method is that it does not cost you anything, except time. There is no overhead and only one sale is required to achieve success. In most circumstances the preference is towards achieving more than one sale.

The targeted number of sales should be enough to pay for the next stage of phased marketing - Flyers / News Papers. If the cost of a 1000 flyer is $40.00, then the target for word of mouth advertising is $40.00 or more. If you prefer a higher number of flyers (suggested) – 10,000 flyers, then the targeted sales figure should be equal to or more than $400.00. This will ensure a seamless process to each and every stage of phased marketing.

Quick Suggestion:-
While writing this, I heard a loud speaker advertising the sale of fish. The salesman goes from village to village plying his trade on a pickup van. He has catchy phrases which highlights the "catch of the day". It seems to work and the villagers gladly use this convenience to get their fishy delights.

With this in mind, it might be fitting to suggest this way of adverting your product. Remember the rule **"the more ears that hear your message the better".** This method will allow word of mouth advertising to be broadcasted to more people. The only limitation is to ensure that it is legal and allowed in your country.

Flyers.
Once you have achieved the required sales/income via word of mouth advertising, it is now time to proceed with next level of phased marketing – flyers. The only purpose of each level is to produce enough income for another stage. If steps are ignored, advertising will result in an expense cycle and become a financial burden. An expense cycle tends to cause a borrowing effect from personal income. The

129

business never learns to support itself or become financially self sufficient.

Remember the rule **"the more ears that hear your message the better"**. The number of flyer distributed is important. For every one hundred flyer you can expect three clients, this is conservative calculation and can be used to gauge the sales to flyer ratio.

Amount required for New Paper Ads is $100.00

1 sales	**=**	**$10.00**
100 flyer =		**3 sales**
approx 400 flyer =		**10 sales**
10 sales	**=**	**$100.00**

Do not limit yourself 400 flyers for the sake of the 100:3 ratio (flyers: Sales), send as much flyers as you can. This will improve the likelihood of success and possibly produce more income. If the response is not forthcoming, change the presentation of the message and continue the distribution. The only goal is to raise $100.00 or more to place newspaper ads.

Hot tips for flyers:-

To conserve money, seek out a friend who is verse on the computer and can do flyers. Reduce the size of the flyers (ensure legibility) so that 3-4 can fit on a long copy page. For each copy page, you will get 4 flyers – this will increase the number of flyer and reduce copy cost.

Newspaper Ads.

The main reason for a stepped process is to enable growth in experience and expertise. It is with this aptitude that a quality sales flow cycle is achieved and the business has the potential of becoming financially self-sufficient. Phased marketing has a deliberate learning curve built in, with each level the brain realign towards better methods of communication. The business and their leaders learn how to advertise to a small group of people and the wider population at large.

If you have not already done so, this is the time to set-up a customer service section in your organization. Why? Remember the rule *"the more ears that hear your message the better"*. Newspapers have a readership in excess of one hundred thousand faithful readers. This means your small ads will be potentially exposed to over 100,000 people. If only one percent responds to your ad, it means that you will receive 500-1000 calls. New business people misunderstand the time it takes to handle this mass of call and fatigue soon set in.

The technique at this stage is to place 3 small classified ads which cost no more that $20.00 - $30.00 each. They should be placed in different sections in the newspaper – health, employment, etc. It will ensure a wide spectrum of the population view that ad.

The call to action should also be concise, instead of says "new computers …call 123 – it should be worded like this – A lightning Fast Laptop, Need One? This creates urgency for the reader and moves the brain into action to satisfy the need.

Did you notice I started the amended ad with the letter A? The reason for this is that newspapers sort their ads in alphabetical order. Any ads starting with any other letter will be sorted alphabetically and reduce the sales potential.

The only reason for these ads is to raise enough money to do radio ads. It does not mean word of mouth advertising or flyer should stop. If your funding permits - do all three, it will certainly increase the chances of success.

It should be noted that you will spend the most amount of time on these three phases, word of mouth, flyers and newspaper ads. Radio ads cost more money to be effective (approximately $1,000.00 - $3,000.00). It is possible to do less than a month's advertising to reduce cost however the results may be lackluster. It is much better to spend the extra time on the first three levels of phased marketing, rather than rush the process and end up in a dangerous expense cycle.

Fiery tips for Newspaper Ads:-

Most businesses handle newspapers ads in the following way, Ads are placed and responses are answered by customer service representative. I suggest you use an "auto responder" – this is an automatic response to any email enquiries. In other words, the ads advertise an email address instead of a phone number. The customer emails for information and receives an automatic response eliminating the representative and any related staff cost.

Radio Ads.

Congratulations! , you have arrived at a very important level of phased marketing, Radio advertisement -the verbal expression of a product. This stage has taken a long time, because it is impractical to directly enter without sufficient money. If resources are limited and there is a rush towards radio ads, it will eat up available monies and drag you "willingly or unwillingly" into an expense cycle.

Throughout this chapter we have discussed the development of a "sales flow cycle". This is the generation of interest income to pay for part of all of the advertising expenses. The ultimate goal of phased marketing is sales gained from little or no start-up capital. If you follow the crowd or the conventional financial gurus, more risk will be taken than is necessary. Phased marketing is not based on risk; it depends on being persistent, practical and having financial aptitude. Before we proceed – remember! , the ONLY goal is to develop a "sales flow cycle" - there should be no other priority.

An effective radio ad or ads are based on one basic principle – the generation of memory via targeted repetition of your message. The biggest mistake people make is trying to cut cost and order less air time. There are so many ads on radio, if your ads is not interesting or lack repetition, the message will get lost in the sea of ads. This results in the wastage of hard earned money and minimal sales.

Phased marketing is based on results and return on investment. Its ultimate goal is to produce profit for a "sales flow cycle". Sales will be generated with one week's worth of radio ads, however branding and memory is difficult. It must be remembered that you have 15-30 seconds to convince a client to purchase a product. A full month's adverting is best way to ensure sufficient sales to cover expenses. The first sale after covering expenses means profit and success.

The tonality and scripting of your ad must invoke one or more of the following:- joy, sadness, concern, urgency, disgust, worry, laughter etc. The ads should have layering of different emotion to evoke a "call to action". Emotions will connect with the listener brain and directly cause a decision to buy. These trigger operate at an unconscious level and influences the "need factor". If a customer is convinced they need your product, sales will take place. Do not be quick to progress to television advertisement; a business can be very success using newspaper and radio advertisement.

If you paid one to three thousand dollars for a month's advertisement, the only goal is to generate enough sales to regain the initial investment. If your product cost one hundred dollars each, the sales needed are between 10-30. Depending on the time of the month these sales are acquired, the choice can be made to pay for additional spots. Every time the expenses are covered seek to get more coverage thus increasing exposure for your product.

Quick Tips for Radio Ads:-

Find a radio station that has the cheapest rates and descent coverage. If production of your ad is done at that station – in most cases production cost is reduced and sometimes free.

The approach I personally use is to generate enough sales to cover the first station's expenses and then move to another station until media coverage spans 5-10 different radio stations. This maximizes exposure while increasing sales and starting the branding process. The continuous aim is to form a quality "sales flow cycle".

Television Ads.

Television ads are expensive, it is not recommended for the faint at heart. The simplest television ads can cost thousands of dollars. If results are less than expected, you can enter into an expense cycle. The upside of television ads is exposure to a product. It generates sales at a much quicker rate than the previous levels of phased marketing.

This is the reason for the development of a quality "sales flow cycle" prior to entering into this level. It is impossible to maintain momentum with limited funds or engage consistent results. The newbie to television advertising gasp at the enormity of the cost and soon revert to cheaper routes. The desire to negotiate better rates is not wrong; however diminishing the budget is not advisable.

Phased marketing is based on the development of a cycle of sales and money. This cycle method creates a "sales flow cycle' and subsequently a quality "interest flow cycle". The interest generated from a "sales flow cycle" add to the budget and results in more and more money to advertise.

The many different concepts and levels of phased marketing are designed to sell your product; its main objective is to create an interest flow cycle. This allows less dependence on sales and progressively redirection into interest income. The concentration on the mechanics of money allow for this very expensive level.

It might seem repetitive I have mention this singular principle in almost every level of phased marketing. The goal is to slowly transform and teach your brain the mechanics of money. If one can understand the true nature of money, a million dollars is possible from a single dollar. Every successful company starts with one dollar; the secret is the understanding of money mechanics and the creation of an efficient business model.

Production.

The creation of a television ad starts with the production of your advertisement. There is nothing cheap about this phase; however it is recommended you get 1-5 quotes from different companies. This will ensure value for your money and allow multiple offers. Do not be afraid to negotiate with your chosen company, if they are willing to provide a quote – a deal / contract is possible. All agreements should be done via contracts and sanctioned by your attorneys. The contract should be worded to protect your interest in the event of a mishap.

It does not matter if your theme is joy, sadness or any other brain triggers the most important thing to do is to feature the product. The advertisement must include color, movement and a simple story – this will ensure the brain attaches to the need response and make a purchase. It also aids in memory and the branding process ultimately leading to sales.

Scheduling Advertisement

It is important to have contracts cover this stage and any other pertinent point of interaction with the company. Market research should be done to determine the most cost effective company providing the most exposure. The main goal of television advertising to create a brand, as such repetition is pivotal.

There is no guarantees your ad will be successful or produce the desired results; however the emphasis is being consistent. Primetime is the ideal timeslot, if it is not available utilize a different time, but keep trying to secure "primetime". It is worth the cost as it leads to branding and automatic sales.

Magic Tips for Television Ads:-
Start with the cheapest station, the goal is to generate enough sales to cover expenses – then repeat with the same station. The process is similar to the staged process of phased marketing; movement is only made when income permits. In this instance, more advertising is only done when sales are generated from the previous ads. If money is made - purchase more, if less money is made – purchase less time. This will achieve consistency and allow the process of branding thus producing easier sales. If the income grows beyond the cost of advertising at station 1, move to the next station (budget permitting). This will ensure an expenses cycle is prevented and a sales flow cycle begins to form.

Main Goals
These are the only goals your business should have when attempting "phased marketing"
- Prevent an Expense Cycle
- Form a Sales Flow Cycle
- Attain an Interest Flow cycle

As we conclude this chapter, it is imperative to internalize the concepts and ensure competency at every level. Information is useless unless it is practically applied. Do not move to a different level of phased marketing unless you emotion, fear level and income allows that movement. This will ensure success, more money and emotional stability.

~ Plan to Fail ~

Chapter 23
Plan to Fail (P2F)

This is by far my favorite chapter. I am proud of all the concepts created but had the most fun writing these expressions of ideas. Why? – You may ask – the reason is that it is so practical and process oriented. My brain gorges itself on the use of the concepts. I am energized by practical and process related things. It can be compared to a roller coaster; my brain enjoys the ride of creating things, processes, efficiencies and being practical. It will not stop unless the goals are achieved in each and every project.

I have spent an immense amount of time in the preceding chapters teaching techniques and principles about making money and now have the audacity to tell you "plan to fail". I would not blame you if a little bit of frustrations sets in, it is only human. The technologies in this chapter may be the exact opposite of what you are presently thinking.

What is P2F? , it sounds like the start of a child's lesson. "P2F" is a technology of planning. A tool used to flourish when things go wrong or fail. It is the process of solving problems at any stage of failure. It is not being positive or trying to make the best out of a situation. Only being positive is like placing a one inch plaster on a ten inch wound or cut. It does nothing but serves as an irritant and may cause more bleeding. There are millions of people worldwide who try to be positive about their situation. The stress manifests itself via sickness, irritability, cursing and many other non-productive emotions. This is the reason for the creation of "P2F".

Businesses worldwide have a backup plan that caters for failure in every aspect of their operations. This is a very good thing and it is strongly recommended to have a detailed plan to cater for mishaps. It is also wisdom to have a "legal" contingency plan in the event or your departure or death. Many businesses fail because the owner thinks they are the end all and be all of the business. The consideration for spouse, children and employees are often overlooked and legal battles ensue for ownership.

P2F starts with the person and gears towards always expecting change to happen. The process teaches the mechanics of solving simple problem which can improve life. It moves into an addiction for solving problems and a celebration for each victory. P2F teaches a thinking process not a backup plan. It has always been my belief, a person who thinks intelligent thoughts will always have successful results. When the thinking process begin to grow in maturity, a business backup plan or problem solving becomes easy. The individual who operates with skill and aptitude generates much admiration from both employees and family.

The problem Addict

Have you ever met a person who speaks only about their problem or the things that are bothering them? There seems to be a dark cloud hovering over their heads and the outlook on life is always negative. The ability to solve problems or enjoy successes is non-existent.

I am sure this is not you, there is no dark cloud over your head and you are not negative. In fact you have past examination, gone to college and now have a position of your dreams. Life is good and there are many successes, family, career and business. How dare I compare you to the "the problem" addict? The person who's problem is infectious and contagious.

It might surprise you how similar your life is to this problem addict. The litmus test is the level of happiness on a daily basis. The excuse might be made that "no one knows what you are going through". We are all given situations to deal with; some people are successful while other isn't. The basic difference is the manner people deal with minor or major problems.

The second misconception is that problem solving comes to us naturally. We attain a certain level of proficiency during the transformation from children into adults. The skill of problem solving is attained through deliberate effort and in most cases NOT a natural occurrence.

The third similarity that exists is your daily speech. If filled with greatness, enthusiasm and joy for life – you have the victory. The reality is we complain, nag, moody and our speech rarely mimic a life of joy. These are only a few examples why people see the "problem addict" in the mirror each morning. There is hope – so keep reading.

Joe's Pencil Collection.

Joe was an aficionado of pencils and collected from every corner of the world. He could identify Spanish made from French, Indian styled from Portuguese and many other permutations and styles. On a rainy afternoon, Joe was admiring his elite collection. A very expensive, one of a kind pencil fell on the ground. Joe screamed in agony, as if he had fallen on the ground. He picked it up carefully, dust it off with the softest feather duster he could find and gentle placed it on the desk. Bradang! It rolled off the table again, repeating the process he placed it on the table, this time changing its position. Due to a tilt on the desk it began to roll even faster. Luckily, Joe caught it in time, placed in the holder and filed alphabetically in his collection. The pencil did not fall this time.

I hoped you enjoyed the story of Joe's silliness; however it teaches the first lesson in P2F – things will always happen. It is therefore the technology or solutions applied which makes the difference. We enjoy peace until one or a group of things goes wrong. The choice is either get flustered or apply solution to problems; sadly the former is the choice of the day.   We live and wire our brains to live in frustration instead of being convinced a solution or solutions always exist. This alone changes our impression and productivity during our daily lives.

How would you solve Joe's silly pencil problem? Think for a minute about the problem – "a pencil falls to the ground" smashing into a million pieces. It is your turn to solve this problem, challenge or difficulty. Try not to look for the right answer, just look for any answer. It is suggested that you come up with a list of solutions, as many creative ways of dealing with Joe's silly problem. The general idea is to re-wire your brain into a solution oriented factory. This simple exercise will begin to open you mind towards carving new directions, instead of stopping at difficulties.

Some people suggested placing the pencil on a table without a slope, while others think leaving it in the holder is the best solution. Another spectrum of the population thought nailing pieces of wood at the end of the table to prevent any pencil from falling. A clever individual indicated viewing of the priceless pencils should be done a cling mat, so it stays in place for inspection.

PROBLEMS X 100 SOLUTIONS = HAPPINESS

There a so many ways of dealing with problem, however at this level of P2F, it is recommended you list at least one hundred solutions. This is a simple way to rewire the brain with the least amount of stress. The reason for listing one hundred or more solutions is to generate the belief and emotional muscle that solutions are possible. Historical beliefs about life sometimes create roadblocks about finding solutions. These negative experiences sprout apprehension about growth and possibilities. It germinates weak willed individual who only see defeat instead of victories.

The list making is a one dimensional approach to P2F. It is finding a solution for a problem and not concerned with creating a habit, procedure or backup plan. At the end of this chapter, it is hoped a habitual backup plan will be a reflex response. There will no longer be a need to plan for mishaps, but it will be an ingrained mode of operation affecting home and business.

SOLUTIONS X 100 = THINKING PROCESS

Jasmine Box Factory.

Jasmine was owner of ABC boxes and had over five hundred faithful customers. Jasmine produced a cheap product that was top quality, this was the reason the business was doing so well. Jasmine had enough workers and did not need to lift a finger but could not keep still. She often joined the workers in the most labor intensive tasks. She never took over the project but submitted to the supervisor to enjoy the hard work.

On this particular day the only job left in the yard was stacking a truckload of wooden crates. Each crate weighed approximately ten pounds each; needless to say Jasmine got a great workout stacking over 200 crates. Jasmine was a peculiar person; she enjoyed seeing thing neat and tidy. It was almost an obsession. Each crate was placed in perfect alignment with the next. Each stack was in exact distance from each other. It was indeed a beautiful thing to behold the exact geometry of such a simple task.

How does stacking crates relate to P2F or the rewiring the brain? Good question! – I can honestly tell you it has nothing to do with wooden crates. It does have a great deal to do with training the brain to think in term of depth and multiple directions. P2F is a technology based on providing the brain with the quickest way to find quality solutions, reduce stress and produce more results.

During our discussion with Joe's silly pencil the job was to master the process of producing a list of solutions and transform from challenges into a solutions environment. This opened the doorway for new pathways in the brain and

142

better methods of doing things. It is the foundation for the next step of P2F – the linking method.

This is a graduation from the previous method; the listing method opens the mind. The linking method provides the foundation for a life based on solution rather than problems. It is not problems do not exist; you just spend less time fussing about feelings and more time solving your situation. P2F is not a lack of emotion but a development of your emotional muscles to face life with a better frame of mind. Being solutions oriented takes more emotions than feeling bad about your situation.

The listing phase involved choosing random solutions to a particular challenge, the linking method deals with creating depth to the process. As the name infers linking can be seen as the structural dimension of P2F. Imagine Jasmine sitting on her neatly stacked crates, underneath her is probably ten to fifteen crates. These crates are real objects; they are not a figment of someone's imagination. The crates support the Jasmine's weight and unless they are there, Jasmine would be sitting on the ground.

The reason for this development stage is to retraining the brain towards problem solving and focus. The skill of focus enhances the speed at which we can efficiently solve a challenge. The process is very simple – think about Jasmine - underneath a crate construct a solution. Ensure the solution is complete and can be use to solve the challenge. Under the first solution, come up with a different solution and mentally place it under the previous. Repeat this procedure until you have linked five to ten solutions underneath main problem. The key is to ensure the solution relates to the problem, is practical and a complete solution. It is wise not to shortcut the solutions as it leads to inefficiency and many unwanted challenges .The following diagram illustrates the linking process:-

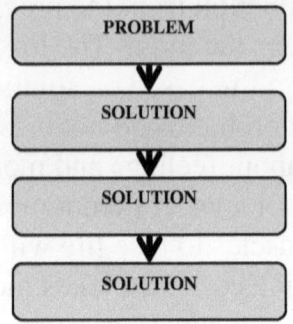

Do not get confused with the explanations or the diagram, the only purpose for these is to generate a mental image of the process. The creation of a pictorial impression allows the brain to use P2F naturally. The linking method teaches the brain to focus on real problems and finds real solution. The listing aspect of P2F will not achieve this measure of understanding. It only opens the gateways for being solution oriented. I wish I could teach you P2F without a stepped process. Our brain will not attach itself anything that is stressful- hence the reason for the procedures.

It is recommended that you identify a problem and practice the linking method until a measure of competence is achieved. Make the solution real and complete until the challenges are easily handled.

Third Stage of P2F.

The third stage of P2F is simple, however it is very effective. It deals with creativity and being response oriented. Listing and linking provided the foundational skills necessary to respond via a reflex rather than a planned thought. This stage generates the muscles needed to produce useful solutions on demand.

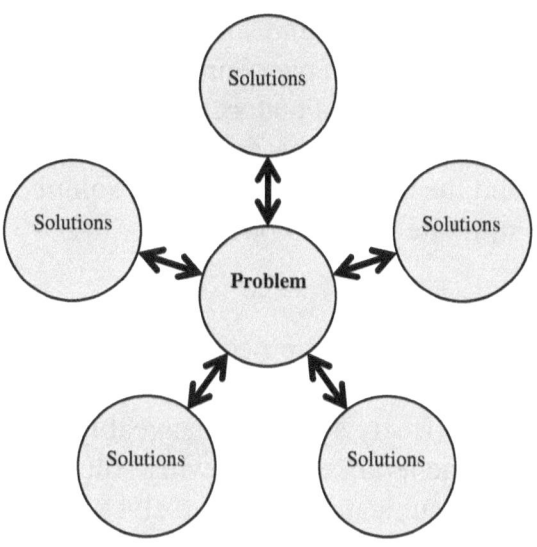

The above diagram illustrates the third concepts of P2F. The communicative and reactive portion of P2F learning curve. I have specifically designed these steps to allow the brain to learn without much effort, if skipped competency and skills will not be achieved. We are not developing a backup plan but a thinking process. This thinking process must be practiced and repeated to form the neural pathways in the brain, the absence of which will cause stress and confusion.

The initial listing phase taught the brain to find solutions, change perspectives and see possibilities. The linking strategy unconsciously forced your brain to focus and matched problem with solution in a structural manner. The process is not apparent at first, but after linking related solutions to a specific problem – the skill of "solution strategies" become part of the brain's way of thinking. Do not get confused with the mechanics of P2F, just remember the pictorial examples of the difference stages. The explanations are there to give insight to the things that are happening in your brain, it is not necessary to memorize.

The third stage of P2F is basically a problem being fed / filled by solutions. A problem that is exposed to continual

145

solutions becomes smaller and smaller. The problem or challenge is attacked from every angle and any challenges arising out of opening the Pandora's Box is handled quickly. The continual bombardment of solutions creates confidence and the ability to find quality solutions. This leads to the ultimate thinking process.

How to use P2F?

Although the teaching process is based on listing, linking and filling – the practical use is not separated. Any stage can be used freely and interchangeably to solve challenges. The general key is allowing solutions to pervade our internal communication with ourselves. Every challenge should follow the guidance of first, second or third stage of P2F or a culmination of all three. Let is look an example:-

- If the car breaks down – you call a tow truck – the truck breaks down – call two wreckers.
- If the cell phone discharges – carry two cell phone – or car chargers
- Trip takes two long – arrange for someone to checking with you at specific times.
- An accident – travel with relatives in two cars
- Food spoilt – identify food places prior to leaving- pack extra food or have on board refrigeration.
- Electricity fail – have backup generator- battery power lights

The scope of this book does not allow for an exhaustive list of solutions and the provision of solutions contradict the essence of P2F. The real power becomes evident as you develop skill. When a person makes a conscious effort to believe solutions exist, they become a *powerhouse of progress*. Prominent dignitaries of the past believed in one singular thought – circumstances could change by applying solutions.

An executive who is in constant contact with a problem will solve, progress and learn from the experience. An individual, who focuses on a problem and ensure solutions are applied will reduce stress and gain life skills. A mother who searches for solutions to manage her stress will be a joy to her children. A father who looks for a job is finding a solution to his poverty or lack of money.

There are so many people around the world who are suffering due to their mindset and the inability to apply quality solutions to problems. You do not have to travel around the world to see this occurrence, look…..or rather listen for your neighbor, how often do they quarrel? If you can hear them, it simple means they have not seen a solution for their circumstance. You do not have to look as far as your neighbors, look at your own family members. If their level of joy is non-existent; they have not learned the skill of solving problems. This set the stage for the forth and final stage of 'P2F' – the happiness level.

Every single concept created is hinged on making the brain happy, without this focus the brain reverts to stress and confusion. Our brain does not know the difference between things that are good for us and those that are bad. It processes information and produces an outcome. It is our conscious decision to take a particular course of action which guides our brain to be led by values or limitation. If a child is given sugar they will be keeping eating the sugar until it is taken away. Our brain is governed by the quantity and quality of stimulus. The more constructive thing we do and think about, the better our lives becomes. The more negative and stressful things we feed our minds – the more our lives digresses.

The reason for the creation of the fourth and final principle is to connect procedures with motivation. Unless an individual is positively motivated, progress becomes arduous and sometimes impossible. The action of "P2F" generates great strides towards improving life. If there is no reason to improve - P2F is useless. We can either focus on our problems or remember our successes. It is a constant awareness that improvements are possible which gives fuel for a better life.

Have you ever noticed how a genuine smile affects people? It breaks tension, causes relaxation and opens the doorway for communication. Our brain seems to enjoy the stimulus of laughter and rushes to find out where it is coming from. The human body is designed to recover or balance off at a level of peace. The body of an accident victim move from injury towards cell, muscles and bone recovery. God has created us to recover from unpleasant situation. The double edge sword is we have been given a free will. This unfortunately is led by the things we feed our brains - negative stimulus produces an unproductive individuals while positive things enables progress.

Fourth / Final Stage of P2F- Happiness.

This stage of P2F celebrates the union between the brain, our bodies and the connection which produces exceptional people. The action of movements appears automatic and natural. There is no planned thought for walking, running or thinking – it just happens. The reality is millions of muscles cells respond to instructions from millions of brain cells. The mind boggling process takes less than a second, however directs the entire body. The mind and body will use what ever method it is given and produce a result. It is our conscious decision that makes it fulfilling.

This is the easiest step of P2F and the most enjoyable. It involves being contented and happy with the solution you have created. The simple action of smiling when a solution comes to mind will generate an addiction to finding solutions. A human being goes towards things that feel good and away from unpleasant situations or feelings. This survival instinct is so strong a person will repeatedly engage in behaviors that bring ecstasy, happiness, peace or joy. We get addicted to those things that feel good or bring

148

"pleasure". We construct our lives to gain as much of those experiences as possible.

The natural survival instinct is the reason the happiness or smiling level of P2F works so well. Let's get started, create a solution to any problem – at the very second the solution comes to mind, smile a little. The idea is to allow the feeling of a smile to fill your heart and chest area. It can be described as a warm sensation that touches you face and quickly envelops your heart. People on this earth know what a smile is and how it feels. Do not try to fake a smile, if the solution pleases you, smile and enjoy it.

The smile or laughter portion of P2F can be applied to the listing, stacking or filling stages and produce excellent results. It will not work if the smile is forced or not genuine. The brain knows when you are not pleased and will make this unpleasant experience. We have learnt from previous chapters the brain always seeks to bring your body away from unpleasant things. As such, the smile must always be filled with joy and happiness.

The reason for the creation of the smiling / happiness phase is to provide motivation for problem solving. If you enjoy solving problems, it becomes an addiction and a continual routine. The routines of our lives are the things which make us happier and progressive. This is the ultimate goal of P2F, solutions, progress, happiness and subsequently a fulfilling life. In conclusion, unless the techniques are used, one will never improve a situation. Make a good choice and improve your life right now!

~ *Strategies* ~

Chapter 24
Strategies!

John Food Stall

John is the village farmer who supplies excellent quality produce to the hundreds of customers who frequent his place. His establishment was designed to highlight both the produce on sale and esthetics of each vegetable section. Green, blue, yellow – all the different permutation of colors could be seen. The focus was to make things attractive to the eyes and comfortable to the brain. In fact – John stall was featured in many newspaper articles and television programs; however it never affected John's humility.

On a pleasant Saturday afternoon, John visited a book store and purchased three of my books:

✓ **How to make more money.**
  Strategies for Financial Freedom.

✓ **Business & Investing.**
  What to do with Money?

✓ **Getting Rich on your present salary.**
  Understanding Money & Wealth.

He read each book carefully and decided to apply the techniques. John visited his local attorney and certified account to get accurate information regarding business registry. He registered his company as – John's Top Quality Fruits Limited. He was very meticulous and made sure the business entity was a limited liability company and not a sole trader- John Doe trading as (TA) John's Top Quality Fruits Limited.

He visited the bank and opened separate accounts for personal and business expenses (opened in the business name). He remembered the rule, *"it is allowed to borrow from the business account to meet personal expenses but*

never *borrow from personal expenses account to pay for business expenses"*. This will ensure a better quality of life for his family and encourage the business to support itself.

His previous bank account had sufficient savings to deposit six (6) times monthly expenses into the personal expense and business accounts. Remembering the petty cash model, he determined to operate personal and business accounts in a similar manner. If $500.00 was spent - $600.00 was returned. Each time the account was reimbursed, an addition $100.-$500. was deposited. This guaranteed growth in each account and an excellent backup plan should things go wrong.

John opened investment accounts which provided 5% interest rate (or more), enabled compounded interest and allowed ad hoc withdrawals/ deposits. John deposited all remaining saving into 2 similar investment account at different financial institutions. The reason for these three investment accounts at different financial institution was spread his risk. The main goal was the formation of a quality interest income cycle. A note pad in hand, John planned his strategy:-

✓ *Open separate account for personal and business expenses.*
✓ *Deposit six times (monthly expenses x 6) in personal and business expenses account.*
✓ *Operate each account like a petty cash system.*
✓ *Open one to three investment accounts in different financial institution.*
✓ *Form a quality interest flow cycle.*

Things were a little fuzzy after that, John and his wife decided to dedicate some more time mastering and internalizing the concepts in my books. You should have seen them go – pen, paper, highlighters, markers, two laptops and a voice recorder. After taking care of the children and spending some quality together, an hour was set aside each day to familiarize themselves with technologies and concept in each book. They repeated and re-read anything that was not fully understood. John and his wife created inventive ways of making the learning process fun – giggling, funny faces, dancing, singing – anything that energized the brain or body. The process worked, it was not long before each of them gains a clear understanding of most, if not all of the concepts outlaid in the books. Making eye contact, simultaneously said – *"back to the business"*, however this time they not only had strategy but knowledge.

Once John was satisfied his family and business accounts were well funded. The only priority thereafter was to form a *"quality sales flow cycle"* and direct all sales to an investment account earning interest income. The interest was small at first, John learned from the books to anticipate this. He stayed consistent and patient and soon a circle of interest began to flow. The interest income was utilized to market his first stall, as the customers increased – so did the balance in the investment account and interest income.

It was not long before all of John's operating expenses were funded by interest income. The additional monies increased both the personal and business balances to twelve times the sum required on a monthly basis. He continued this trend until these balances grew so large it needed an investment account of its own. The cycle of interest income and balance increases were repeated over and over again and has not stopped to this day.

During lunch, John gazed at the wind blowing the trees tops and began thinking to himself, this is so easy. I have not spent a dime of my money and have amassed such a large bank balance. I could stop selling and it would not affect my way of life. Why is it that other people don't do this? Drawing reference from my books, John remembers a quote *"historical financial beliefs are the hardest thing to change"*. It was true; most people work hard and never understand the mechanics of money. They leave large balances in low interest accounts creating a dangerous expenses cycle.

Lovingly his wife asked – do you remember what an expense cycle is? Snickering (lovingly) back, he replied – do you remember why an expenses cycle is so dangerous? Trying to compete with each and pretending to be in a classroom - John raised his hand. Miss, miss! Yes John, replied his wife – well said John; an expense cycle is using any money earned to support a family or business. The money is used up and a treadmill experience of continually working to get money develops. There is no recurring benefit from any money that is earned; it simple disappears after it is spent.

It is your turn replied John, why is an expense cycle so dangerous? His wife calmly sat down, adjusted her clothing and crossed her legs in a teasing fashion. An expenses cycle is dangerous because it creates too many variables and money earned camouflages these variables / problems. The activity of employment or business creates money and used to support the family or business. If the breadwinner or business owner is taken out of the picture, the "activity income" is reduced or disappears.

In the family situation, the lack of income cause unexpected financial hardship for the spouse and children. A business expenses cycle is twice as dangerous as money hides inflationary cost that can cause a business to tailspin into unexpected debt. When money solves business problems, the awareness of their bank balance is skewed and becomes unrealistic. The use of money to cover financial bumps, depletes resources and creates a dependence of spending. This spending cements an expense cycle and can cause many unseen financial danger and mistakes.

After pretending to be teacher and student, they collected themselves and decided to use their newfound tools and knowledge to grow the business in a much better manner. The first stall proved to be very successful; a decision was made to open another stall. The same modus operandi was adopted for the new stall, the development of a quality interest flow cycle which provided interest income to support expenses.

The remaining interest income from the new stalls was added to the investment portfolio of the original vegetable paradise. There was a continual increase in the balance and subsequently interest income. This process was repeated until John and his wife owned one hundred stalls in key areas of the country. The interesting fact was after the tenth stall, interest income grew so large John was able to open each store faster and faster.

The last I heard of John's family was a grand celebration for the thousandth stall and a chain of organic vegetable mega stores. John business model has not changed to date. He still follows the same interest income strategy and has not spent a dime of his earned money. The only focus is to grow his investment balance thus producing a quality interest income cycle. John is not worried any more, if sales are made the interest income is always available to market his business and produce more interest income.

I received an email from John recently; he was very appreciative for the simplistic approach to finance. They have purchased many luxuries in life and living comfortably, but the most important thing they have learnt is to stay humble and keep learning.

Amanda Apartments
Amanda was a beautiful twenty year old diva who had the curves to prove it. She wore the latest designs and although sometimes revealing was always classy and tasteful. Needless to say, the boys of the neighborhood took notice and vocalized their expression of lust, love or admiration. She was never ruffled and handled it with poise, patience and composure. Amanda had a talent for dressing

155

but to the surprise of those boisterous males, she was a strewed proprietor and an intelligent soul.

After work on a Friday afternoon, Amanda needed a clothing 'fix' and visited the nearby mega mall emporium. The credit card swiped faster and faster racking up thousands of dollars for numerous pieces of clothing. Bag around her neck, hand and any human hanging place she could find. The bags were packed in the car faster than a speeding bullet. Remembering to pick up a book for her niece's birthday, a visit was made to a popular book store. While rummaging through the CD section she came across one of my products:-

☺ **How to make more money.**
   Strategies for Financial Freedom.
   (Audio Seminar - CDs)

She made the purchase and decided to listen to the CDs on her journey home. The expectations for the seminar/audio version of *"How to make More Money- Strategies for Financial Freedom"* were neutral and she kept an opened mind. The most interest thing was the simplicity of the principles. It took advanced financial concepts and presented them in an *"easy to understand"* format. Any and everyone who took some time to learn the principles could transform a dollar in their pocket into a fortune. She stopped her car an listed the principles

✓ IFC™ – Interest Flow Cycle ™.
Income placed into an investment account/s to produce a continual flow of interest income.

✓ Expense Cycle ™
The use of earned income to support a family or business, when the activity that produces the money disappears, so does the income. It also creates a need to always be working to earn money.

Amanda remembered from the CDs, learning comes by repetition and being continually exposed to the information. She made a decision there and then to dedicate one hour daily (2-4 weeks) to internalize and master the information. She did it! The awareness and practicality of interest income soon became clear and real, it was time to change Amanda apartments.

The apartment's rental agreement was between Amanda and the tenants; she visited the local government office and registered the business as Amanda Apartments Limited. As with Joe, care was taken to ensure the type of business entity was Limited Liability Company. The rental agreement was resigned under the business name and the existing tenants. An account was opened for personal expenses. A business bank account was opened in the company's name "Amanda Apartments Limited". Sufficient deposits were made in each account to cater for six times the sum needed for personal and business expenses. The same petty cash model was adopted, if $1,000.00 was spent - $1,100.00 was deposited at month end.

A visit was made to her local tax professional to ensure compliance with relevant tax codes in her country. Consultation was made with the fire service and the government building code department to ensure that all structures and safety items were in accordance to the law of the land.

It was time to convert "Amanda Apartments Limited" into a business powerhouse. Amanda's only focus for the next year was to create a "quality interest flow cycle". A concerted effort was made to ensure the business expenses was well funded to cater for unexpected emergencies and effectively run the business. The next step was to funnel any excess cash into an investment account that produced five percent or more in interest income. The interest income was very small at first, however Amanda learnt this should be the only priority after funding her expense accounts. The simple idea was to slowly replace part or all of the business expenses with interest income forming a "quality interest income cycle".

After the first six months results were beginning to show, interest income was paying for her business expenses and no money earned was being spent. This excited Amanda, she cranked up the deposits and the interest income soon obliterated her expenses. The portfolio of investments (compounded interest accounts) generated so much additional interest; Amanda bought another property. The interest income from the previous rental was used to pay the mortgage installment. The new rental property was initially supported by the previous; however it was not long before the new rental supported itself via interest income. The excess interest income was funneled back into the original investment account increasing the balance and subsequently the interest income.

Amanda Apartments Limited soon blossomed into five hundred rental properties. It was time to put some financial legs under her company. She had learnt from my CDs that a vast majority of companies make the mistake of following a singular financial line. In the case of Amanda Apartments Limited, money was only being generated from rental income. As such only one leg was holding up her financial table. Although her business was well funded and even if all her apartments were lost, interest income will still support her lifestyle. The development of a quality interest flow cycle would plateau or be maxed out.

She added five star restaurants to each of the five hundred rental properties. This was second leg under the financial table, however from an investment perspective left a shaky portfolio. The interest income from these two sectors of Amanda Apartments Limited was substantial enough to open her dream company – Amanda clothing International Limited. This place a third leg under the financial table and created interest income stability, however it was a table with three legs and still somewhat

158

unstable. As the company grew, the interest income also grew and sectors of the business opened faster and faster.

The clothing company was split into five sections - clothing, ladies bag, underwear, shoes and bridal gowns. Along with the restaurants at each rental, enough land was available to open Amanda's Mega Malls. This attracted droves of people cementing and extending the Amanda's brand. The changes added more and more legs under the financial table. The financial table became so strong financially that no monetary variable shook the company.

I saw a full page advertisement displaying another financial leg of Amanda Group of companies – Amanda Five Star Hotels Limited. Not bad for a beautiful twenty year old diva who loved to dress.

Global Enterprises

Global Enterprises is a successful company with over one thousand branches worldwide. Mark is the founder and built the company with one hundred dollars in his pocket. The company now generates five millions dollars on a monthly basis and employs over one thousand employees. At the surface Global Enterprises appears to be financially sound and poised to grow exponentially.

The reason for the fantastic growth is the founder's willingness to be open and learn new information. He attended one of my seminars and learnt about the business expenses cycle, variables they create and reasons they are so dangerous. Mark reviewed the seminar information over and over again until a level of proficiency was achieved. During his flight back to his office, he listed the pertinent points taught at the seminar.

- *Expense Cycle* ™
  Business profit (from sales) used to grow and expand an organization. When the activity of business is gone or sales decreases, profit drops and can result in a large organizations becoming financially unstable.

- *Variables*

An organization use of capital money (money earned from sales) to solves financial problems. When problems are covered up or solved by money, the more *"profit"* become dependant on those solutions. This simple process create numerous expense cycle "type" variable and hides the companies true profitability. In other words when the director sees the bank balance, they think it is profit – however it is actually:-

Profit – Variables = Bank Balance.

- *Why an Expense Cycle ™ is dangerous?*

An expense cycle creates a dependence on the profit to carry on the business. If there was no company, there would be no money. Solving problems with money creates too many variables and profit becomes overburdened with spending. This causes more variable and further cements the company into an expenses cycle. The dangers translate themselves into any new branch or company that is opened. It acts like a virus devouring resources at lightning speeds. In effect a company who is addicted to an expense cycle looks like this

**Expense Cycle ™ x Variables = Expense Cycle ™ = More
Variables**

Profit = More Variables

After making notes on his laptop, Mark heard an announcement from the pilot *"Ladies and gentlemen we are cruising at 35,000 feet and will arrive at our destination on schedule"*. Mark looked at his watch and knew it about two hour before landing. It was time to do some planning and make critical changes in Global Enterprises.

Mark emailed his directors and mangers regarding an emergency meeting. At five o'clock sharp the next day, the

160

room was soon filled with all senior officials of the company. It was ablaze with chatter and curiosity; each person wondered the purpose for such an urgent meeting. Mark stepped into the board room and you could have heard a pin drop. What could this be about?

The founder and CEO anticipated the tension brewing prior to his arrival. He planned to break the "ice" with a toast to the success of the company and the many strides each director and manager achieved. Seconds after Mark's arrival, waiters entered the room with glasses of champagne. The CEO stood up, raised his glass and said, *"I am truly thankful for each of you sitting in this room today and am confident it is your hard work that caused Global Enterprises success"*. The gesture germinated instantaneous smiles and laughter quickly filled the board room. While Mark was genuine about his commendations, the distraction worked and everyone was relaxed and open to new information.

The wise CEO recounted the seminar and information presented, he made reference to Global Enterprises addiction to an expenses cycle, profit variables and the illusion of financials stability. Mark dissected the company financials, clearly showing the real bank balance (net profit less variables). A slide show was used to show profitability due to sales and the resulting effect if those income streams were impeded.

He reiterated how quickly a company would enter into financial difficulties if the activity of a manager, production or sales stopped. The five million dollars in monthly profit became smaller and smaller as the meeting progressed. All directors and mangers agreed drastic change was needed to safeguard the wealth of the company.

Mark first course of action was the training of all top officials at the company. Daily training sessions were held until everyone had tools to improve their personal finances and make better decision for the company. The following changes took places in less than a month:-

161

Step 1

- Central accounts were opened for each sector of the company; six times the monthly operating expense was transferred to each account. This shifted monetary linage from head office forcing performance in each sector. The sectors were still monitored; however the purpose was achieve a sales flow cycle and subsequently an interest flow cycle in every sector. The same petty cash model was adopted for the reimbursement of any monies spent.

Step 2

- Investment accounts were open for each sector and excess monies were funneled into these account. The interest generated was small at the start however quickly grew to encompass all operating expense of that particular sector. A sales flow cycle was soon developed which led to a quality interest flow cycle. Any excess interest was forwarded an investment account at the head office, thus growing the balance and subsequent interest income. The new income was used to open additional branch and the same process was repeated.

The company's financials were monitored closely, its main goal was interest income and not spending any earned money. The company grew even faster than before cementing its position in the global economy. Mark not only ran the companies on interest income but had an excellent monetary plan should thing go wrong. Mark started off his business with very little; nothing is stopping you from doing the same!

162

Susan the Web Master

Susan did not do well in school but had a natural talent for webpage design and was very internet savvy. She tried many ideas, however never seem to be making a consistent profit from online adventures. Profit seems to be absorbed into advertising the business and some months even ran at a loss. She knew money could be made on the internet; however encountered great difficulties getting off the ground.

A friend who had success with one of my books *"How to Make More Money – Strategies for Financial Freedom"* knew about Susan's plight and agreed to lend the book, with one condition. Susan must master the concepts or pay a thousand dollars to her friend -the bet was on!

Susan was a very competitive individual; failure was not part of her vocabulary. She took on the challenge and was determined not to lose the bet. An entire month was utilized to study the book. If anything was not clear a second or third reading was done. The information was repeated until she could visualize / dissect any company into their monetary systems. Practice, practice and more practice was the goal of the second month. A high standard was set for the internalization, understanding and competency of the concepts.

While sitting at a popular fry chicken restaurant Susan began to analyze the cash flow models and wrote the following:-

BUSINESS PLACE + EMPLOYEES + FRY CHICKEN = MONEY

EXPENSES = MONEY

....

MORE EXPENSES = MORE MONEY

....

NO EXPENSES = NO MONEY

NO BUSINESS PLACE = NO MONEY

NO EMPLOYEES = NO MONEY

The first observation was an expense cycle, if the company did not make money there would be no resources to pay for expenses. It was clear that three variables produced money for the restaurant and without these money would not exist. If there was a public health issue sales would come to a screeching halt and threaten the survival of the business.

Susan thought for a moment, how can this business model be fixed? She wrote a new set of equations:-

BUSINESS PLACE + EMPLOYEES + FRY CHICKEN = MONEY

EXPENSES = MONEY

....

MONEY + INVESTMENTS = INTEREST INCOME

....

164

INTEREST INCOME + MORE DEPOSITS X TIME = MORE INTEREST

....

INTEREST INCOME = BUSINESS PLACE + EMPLOYEES = FRY CHICKEN

....
....
MORE FRY CHICKEN = MORE INTEREST INCOME

The new equations corrected the expense cycle of the business and would have made it less and less dependent on sales. Additional sales increased the balance of the investment portfolio and subsequently the interest income. A decision could now be taken to pay part or all of the business operating expenses from interest income. Sadly this equation was only in Susan's head and not a reality for the fry chicken restaurant. When a business runs on an expense cycle, it is so easy for it to lose income and risk closure.

After this monumental fry chicken experience Susan return home and wrote down some changes for her internet business.

- Register business a limited liability company.
- Open separate accounts and funds them with 3-6 times the monthly expenses needed
- Operated each account using the petty cash system , if $5000.00 was utilized – a sum of $5,200.00 was returned to the account
- Set up investment accounts accruing 5% or more interest and funnel all excess income into them.

The changes were made, however a decision was taken to purchase software that aided in ranking her website on all major search engines. It took some time but a staff of ten

165

was soon hired to check ranking, send out emails and add incoming/outgoing linkages to the websites.

The website began to get better ranking placement and attracted free visitors. At first, only one hundred clicks were received per day. As more linkages were added the visitors increased to over one million and the actual click through was one hundred thousand.

The reason for all this effort was making money without spending a dime on advertising. The book taught her that income should never be too dependent on numerous variables. She creates her personal equations and applied it stringently to her internet business:-

INTERNET BUSINESS + WEBSITE RANKING = MONEY

....

PAID ADVERTISMENT + FREE VISITORS = MORE MONEY

....

MORE MONEY = INTEREST INCOME = MORE ADVERTISING

....

MORE ADVERTTISING + FREE VISITOR = MORE INTEREST

....

MORE INTEREST + MORE INTEREST + FREE VISITORS= MILLIONS

Although the business started off on an expense cycle, deliberate effort and persistence created a quality interest income cycle. Sales were acquired from both free visitors and paid advertisement which slowly eliminated the variables needed to make money. At present Susan's only focus was to increase the balance of the investment portfolios and interest income. She remembered wealth is measured in interest income and not the bank balance. The purpose of the bank balance is three-fold – interest, retention of all sales income and an excellent backup plan in the event of emergencies.

The cycle of free visitors produced sales without overhead, the money earned was used to pay for more advertising. As the advertising increased so did the sales. The company was able to afford additional staffing for ranking websites. It was not very long before Susan had one thousand websites holding top ranking on all major search engines. Customers searching for related topics found Susan's websites listed first. The placement produced millions of sales at no cost to the company.

Susan remembered a pertinent concept from studying the book. *Income must never depend on an expense cycle or too many variables.* Ranking websites never stopped, however being an astute internet mogul Susan needed to progressively correct her monetary equations. The income was converted to follow a new model:-

INTEREST INCOME = RANKING + PAID ADVERTISMENT

The correction was made to ensure all business activities would be dependent on interest income only. All monies were used to increase interest, this meant Susan hardly ever spent any of her capital or earned income.

Susan's friend visited my office recently and relayed the fantastic success story. An email was also received from Susan explaining her gratitude for the information. My reply to her email was as follows:-

Good Day Susan,

Thanks for your wonderful email and kind words of encouragement.

Please be reminded my book was a tool that pointed in a new direction.

167

It was your deliberate effort, persistence and willingness to be open-minded which created your success.

We are all given wings to fly and it is up to us to make the choice to take flight.

Best Regards

Curtis Siewdass

Susan invited her friend to dinner and gloated about winning the bet. They had a nice laugh; Susan received a thousand dollars and knew from that day life would always have the potential of getting better. She wrote a note and slid it across the table – *life is about happiness, joy, laughter and fulfillment.*

It is important to master the concepts in this book, be open minded and always seek to improve your life spiritually, emotionally and financially.

Your
~ Global Business
~

Chapter 25
How to See Your Global Business?

Global expansion is the goal of most companies. In today's world import and export has become very easy. Most countries have licensed brokers who take care of all respective documentations for shipping and export. There are thousands of courier companies worldwide who collect packages from your doorstep and deliver to customers. The industry has become so competitive prices have been driven very low. The problem is not the shipping itself but the protection and sustainability of the exporter.

The internet has made a global business even easier. A person selling computers in Japan can now connect with potential customer in Alaska. The increasing numbers of people going online daily is mind boggling. This sets the stage for millions of potential customers. Advertising companies on the internet have designed their systems to be user-friendly and very cost effective. This means anyone can advertise anything at anytime and incur minimal cost. There is also a term used by these advertising companies which is geographical targeting. This is the ability to target a specific country, state or region for potential customers.

A company distributing products abroad must consider legal and intellectual property rights:-

Legal

Any company doing business anywhere should be registered as a limited liability company. Business entities differ from country to country and the type of registration required may be different. The type of entity chosen *must* offer legal protection for the owners. It is important to seek legal counsel in your local and destination country to ensure comprehensive legal protection.

Intellectual Property Right

This is involves following specific rules laid down by local government and international treaties for the protection of inventions and creative works. There are many considerations for protecting intellectual property. The scope of this book does not permit a complete guide or listing. As previously mentioned, seek legal advice for the registration of Patents, copy rights and trademarks (etc). This will prevent or minimize unauthorized duplication of your work or products.

A proper financial foundation is important for a business to expand globally. It is assumed they are well equipped to manage the cost for export. The reality is companies rely on an expenses cycle for global trade. This is the use is sales income to support related expenses. If sales do not occur there is no export and subsequently no income.

The major lesson taught in this book is to never operate a business (long term) on an expenses cycle or have income dependant on too many variables. Sadly, a large percentage of businesses worldwide follow the expense cycle model and find themselves scrambling to pay export costs. The variables are not recognized as money solves these problems. It is only when emergencies happens financial dangers are revealed. It is hard for a seasoned business person to admit their income is based on an expenses cycle or variables. They may have been making money like this for a very long time and may not agree with these monetary dangers.

The visible evidence of an expense cycle is the recession each country is presently facing. Business people were never taught about these concepts and built mega businesses on the flow of sales income. The crash of the America's economy revealed the lack of financial stability in global businesses. The domino effect was the closure and bankruptcy of many longstanding companies. These institutions were icons for decades and in a matter of weeks depleted cash resources. The unfortunate occurrence was the retrenchment of millions of workers and unexpected hardship for their families.

A business risk many challenges however can make an immense amount of money by going global. The money enhances the lives of directors, managers and employees. A company starts with ten employees; global expansion requires a large amount of staff. The number may be in the hundreds or even thousands allowing employment to a wide cross section of the world's population. Global expansion will positively affect the country, its people and region's economic environment.

An investigation into the monetary construct of companies revealed many successes. It also highlights fatal flaws in day daily operations which go unseen. These deficiencies are not visible because money covers problem. This false impression festers within the financial foundations of the business. It erupts when there is a shortage of money and aggressively consumes visible *(available money)* cash flow streams.

How should a business approach export / global expansion? The answer follows the same principles taught in this book, the development of sales and interest flow cycle. The basic concept is conversation from an asset base model into a monetary model, thus allowing money to make money. The conversion process forces a business to be based on cash resources and not the net worth of their assets. It is easier to move around money than a five story building.

Use the Internet
Advertising on the internet allows a company to expand globally with little or no overhead.

Optimize the Website to received free advertising

Optimization is simple formatting internal coding of a website for better recognition by search engines. It requires related inbound links – similar website placing a link to your website on their webpage. As the number of links increases the ranking of your website also increase. These process places your website on the first 3 pages of any web search. It is seen be millions of potential customers for **FREE**. The downside is it takes time and basic programming knowledge. The payoff of free advertising is definitely worth the effort.

Match Advertising with Sales (Sales Flow Cycle)

The sales should form a base for the payment of advertising cost. The coverage of internet cost should then lead to local advertising (newspapers, radio, television etc) – always maintain a sales flow cycle. The income derived from paid and free advertising is used to form a circle of sales and income. It is then linked to an investment portfolio for interest income. The paid and free advertising increases the balance of the portfolio and subsequently dominance in the markets.

Start Small – Grow in Stages

Global expansion should only take place as the interest income increase. This will allow for unencumbered growth of the organization.

Seek legal Council

Always ensure that you are guide by the appropriate and competent legal council to ensure compliance with the laws of the land.

Global expansion has been become much easier than previous years. While the process is simpler for import and export, if the financial are not understood losses will occur.

173

The interest income cycle explained in this book in an excellent tool for any business operation. It does not focus on the activity of making money but allowing money to be the driving force for wealth. I have learnt knowledge is the key for any progress but competent knowledge produce money, riches, wealth and personal fulfillment.

Chapter 26
Bonus Chapter
The Power of Processes
Process Flow Cycle.

Have you ever gone to a popular business place and was appalled by the customer service or bought a product that did not meet your expectation. We all encountered these problems at one time or the other. These deficiencies exist both in the private and government sectors. There are so many companies that fit this description; it has become the norm rather than the exception.

On the other end of the spectrum are those companies which never disappoint and provide quality products with amazing customer service. They make you feel like a person rather a dollar bill.

I have always been curious why some companies are great and others fall way behind. The grass root things causing success or failure or magic seeds for the exceptional organizations. Efforts to find a unique road map for greatness yielded varying opinions. In order to bridge the gap something had to be created that transcend companies and personal preferences. Technologies that could be easily applied and produce more results. This is the reason for the creation of the *"process flow cycle"*.

The Problem.

A company's name is the description or representation of business. It is how they are known to public and a means by which products are recognized. Employees described themselves as (ABC workers or XYZ workers etc) or they are working for ABC Company or XYZ Company. The employee is not described to the public; it is the company who makes the connection. A classic example – a worker calls another organization and says *"Good Morning Mr.*

Mark, I am calling from XYZ Company". The company is recognized not necessarily the worker. This is the reason organizations spend so much time, money and effort safeguarding their reputation.

The problem begins when the collective intelligence of the company is viewed as the intelligence of a specific employee, supervisor, director or CEO. It is assumed the higher the position, the better the ability to generate efficiencies, solve problems or be stress free. The assumption is off-base and much further from policies than is realized.

People interpret things in different ways and are instigator of bureaucracies and longwinded processes. They mistake structure for efficiency and routines for 'best practices'. A close-minded approach is developed over time and inventive thinking is replaced by stagnated policies.

It is assumed these individuals also manage their personal challenges with the same efficiencies. The reality is employee seldom mimic emotional success or progress in their lives. The deficiencies are translated into the company's policies and results in many delays. Customer service, decision making and numerous internal connections are affected. This slows the company's ability to grow or expand its operations.

The leaders create policies to handle the needs of the organization; the ingrained behaviors find their way into the processes and inadvertently cause delays. The inconveniences directly affect the goodwill and reputation of the company.

The problems of learnt structure is experienced however not always visible. The tangible evidence is seen in long lines. Yes; long lines – these lines may signify the popularity of the company, but is a clear indication of inadequate processes. Every time a line is seen it represents a policy or process that was born on the board room table. It sounded intellectually good, however the application of the process was not clearly investigated. The delays are sometimes ignored and can turn away customers.

Individuals also choose processes that are inefficient. They find a way of doing something and follow that routine religiously. It does not matter if it takes too long, expensive, not produce results or make things worse. The routine does not change and soon become a reality of life which is extremely difficult to the change.

Process Flow Cycle

PFC
Process Flow Cycle ™

The process flow cycle is a simple tool which reduces time while producing progressive efficiencies. It is a mechanism of slowly identifying deficiencies and transforming them into positive results. The model is designed to be easily implemented and speed up the learning curve for change.

How does it work?

It works by indentifying the process, decide the goal and use the model to slowly change. ***An open mind is imperative for use of the Process Flow Cycle*** .If the goal is not better results or greater efficiency, this model will be useless.

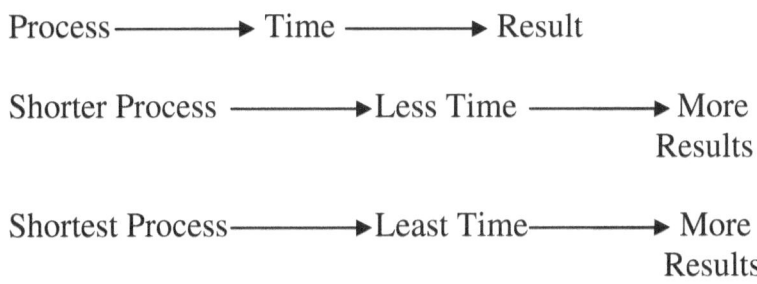

Process ——————→ Time ——————→ Result

Shorter Process ——————→ Less Time ——————→ More Results

Shortest Process——————→ Least Time——————→ More Results

177

The above model illustrates the 'process flow cycle'. It reveals that processes can improve by the reduction in the number of steps. As the process get smaller and smaller, so does the time needed for its completion. The product or service that is offered to the public is positively affected.

The process flow cycle mimic the way the brain works and attempts to easily create efficiency. Our brain learns to do things by repetition, when the skill is learnt the process is shortened to reduce stress. The goal of our brain is not efficiencies; the aim is to reduce stress. The byproduct of this process is efficiency. As the individual focus on the skill, the brain automatically shortens the process reducing time needed for the task.

We constantly practice the process flow cycle, albeit that we are unaware of its use. A driver who is transferred to a different location will initially learn one way to get to and from work. The person eventually learns many different ways to reach their destination. The directions are stored and the brain automatically calculates the shortest and most efficient route. This is the premise on which the process flow cycle is based, the brain continual struggle to reduce stress and find equilibrium.

Step 1
Do not accept your present modus operandi as the rule of law.

An individual or company who is not open-minded will never want to see the benefits of the process flow cycle. They will defend the present processes at the expense of customer service. The main reason is due to the *"comfort level equation"*

COMFORT LEVEL = ROUTINE = NO CHANGE

The comfort level of any situation generates routine. This way of doing things cycles a comfort level. It is very difficult to change historical beliefs or mindsets, they war against any changes. Strangely enough, the defenders of the routines and comfort levels may not realize their own behaviors. The major reason is *"if it works – why change it?"*. The process flow cycle is meaningless if the users are not willing to question their present way of doing things.

Step 2 -
Read over Step 1
Do not accept your present modus operandi as the rule of law.

It has been my observation people adopt an intellectual understanding of process improvement. Only having a mental understanding carries many hindrances or burdens. An individual thinks they are being open minded but makes decision from old beliefs. It is very important to ensure you are truly being opened minded for the process flow cycle to work.

Step 3 -
Identify and break apart the process

An investigation of the true process of any operation is imperative. It is not recommended to cut corners at this stage. Trying to save face or prevent embarrassment will not produce the desired result. Take some time and clearly identify the process (eg. Customer service process, accounting process etc). The next step is to list the process via a flow chart

© Curtis Siewdass 2009

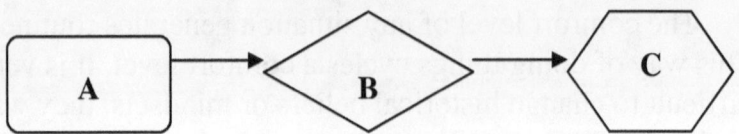

A = Customer Enters the Door
B = Customer Arrives at the counter
C = Customer fills out form etc

If this methods seems too difficult for you, simple create a list which indentifies aspects of the process. The reason I prefer diagrams or pictures is to create an image for the brain to be attached and a base for memory. An individual may opt to break apart the processes via the use of small circles that connected. Whichever way that is chosen, the purpose is to clearly see the process on paper and create a road map for the procedure.

It is also important to discuss the validity or trueness of each part of the process. An honest review will create an excellent foundation to realistically show how well the process works or its deficiencies.

Step 4 -
Question each part of the process.

This is the most difficult thing follow. Laid down procedure represent years of routines and asking for changes is not always easy. People become defensive and attempt to explain reason for the process to stay. Ask the following question when trying to ascertain the relevance of a part of the process.

- How much time is this step adding to the process?
- Is this step necessary?
- Can this step be amended, change or replaced?

- Can policies be changed to amended, change or replace parts of the process?
- Are we trying to defend this part of the process or create efficient changes?

Step 5 -
Make the entire process shorter over time.

The above explanations are designed to eliminate any bias attached to a process. The final step is the easiest; it is the reduction of a process into fewer parts. If the dissection of the original process entailed fifteen different parts, the *process flow cycle* is the reduction of these procedures. Steps are not eliminated for nonsensical reasons; changes only take place if value is added to the process.

In order for the **process flow cycle** to work, the goal must be to continually reduce the steps it takes to complete a particular task. The continual use of the *process flow cycles* creates a certain level of skill in making processes shorter and more efficient. A critical eye is developed for the creation of efficiencies. An individual is able to see process improvements in their personal and work lives. Companies using the *process flow cycle* improves customer service, production capabilities and human resources. This is due to the universal application of the *process flow cycle* to any spectrum of a company.

Once the basics are understood the process flow cycle will question the foundations of any business. The mechanics of *the process flow cycle* will create policy and procedural changes in a company. The true meaning of efficiencies will manifest itself by the generation of more income.

As we concluded this chapter, it is recommended that the *process flow cycle* be practiced on simple things before graduation to monetary models. Improvement could be made for cleaning your home, yard or car. It is simple looking at the manner things are done and attempt to produce more results in less time. These simple examples are free and only cost practice. The practices will yield skill which can be use to improve company processes and subsequently make more money.

~ *Conclusion* ~

Chapter 27
Conclusion

Congratulations, you not only read this book but mastered the concept taught. It is hoped these simplistic principles have opened your mind to the mechanics of money. As we conclude our conversations, you should be competently aware of the following

- ✓ **Expense Cycle**
- ✓ **Interest Flow Cycle.**
- ✓ **Sales Flow Cycle**
- ✓ **Process Flow Cycle**

When these technologies are applied stringently, it results in a transformation of personal and business finance and ultimately wealth. After all this impartation of knowledge it normal to assume this book might end with a grand investment strategy however there is one more cycle I desire to teach. This strategy transcends economies, money, wealth and financial status.

During biblical times God's people were instructed to build enormous storehouses for grain and other food items. These backup plans catered for drought and hardship. Our present 'technologically advanced" world depend on the value of money and the ability of their government to keep the financial wheels spinning. This present recession (2008-2009) highlighted how quickly companies become bankrupt and people lose jobs. A lesson to be learnt is there are limitations to the value of money and it affect the rich and those living in poverty.

In the event of an emergency import, export, utilities, and security (etc) are all affected. These vitals may not resume immediately and providing for families becomes difficult. Simply put, the value of money in your bank account will be meaningless. Most governments worldwide are only interested in collecting or making money, there do not have any food related backup plan should an emergency arise. Everyone depends on groceries for food.

The last cycle I want to teach is a **"Food Flow Cycle"**. This is the utilization of your present interest income to purchase a stock of food that can comfortable last for (2-3 months). It works the same as the petty cash model taught earlier. If food stores dip below a certain level, new purchases are made ensuring extra food is purchased.

A family may opt to use the excess food or donate to charity, however must ensure new purchases are made first. This measure will guarantee your family will be provided for in the event of an emergency. Statistically, most catastrophic situation begins to improve after the first month. A food flow cycle will provide a backup plan until things return to normal.

Remember money does not purchase intelligence; it is your deliberate effort which produces knowledge, progress and happiness. Thank you for taking the time to speak with me and completing this journey. It is hoped the technologies in my book will be a catalyst for financial stability and success in your life. God Bless you and your family. Wishing you great and continual success.

~ *Epilogue* ~

Epilogue

Curtis Siewdass was born to humble beginnings, taking care of cattle for the first twenty years of his life. It was a hard and arduous task, however developed physical and emotional strength. The times spent in the pastures modeled his brain into being curious about how things worked. Needless to say an obsession was developed.

He has been a born again Christian for the past twenty four years, holding the position of an elder and passionate about improving people's lives via God's word.

He attained a fourth degree black belt (4th Dan) in martial arts, the skill acquired cemented the ability to dissect processes into their singular entities and rearrange into efficient foundations.

Curtis has over ten year in the financial sector; however his personal hobby is financial strategy. He created four concepts Expense Cycle, Interest Flow Cycle, Sales Flow Cycle and Process Flow Cycle. Its purpose is to convert personal and business finance into progressive and successful entities. Curtis is also the author of the following books:-

Financial
- How To Make More Money – Strategies Financial Freedom
- Business and Investing - What to Do with Money (publish date Dec 2010).
- Getting Rich on Your Present Salary – Guide to Money and Wealth. (publish date Dec 2010)

Motivational
- Fixing Life's Problems – Guide to Emotional Freedom. (publish date Dec 2010)

Fitness
- Your Health – Fact & Fiction - Getting it Right

Curtis believes any situation can improve once people are willing to be open minded and goal oriented. The purpose in life should always be personal happiness and a deliberate catalyst for happiness in others.

Want to listen to Live
Seminars online?

Visit our Website

www.topmoneyplan.com

www.ingramcontent.com/pod-product-compliance
Lightning Source LLC
Chambersburg PA
CBHW032008170526
45157CB00002B/600